AF589273

ABDA STRIKING FORCE 1942

The joint Allied command lost at Java Sea

Angus Konstam
Illustrated by Adam Tooby

OSPREY PUBLISHING
Bloomsbury Publishing Plc
Kemp House, Chawley Park, Cumnor Hill, Oxford OX2 9PH, UK
Bloomsbury Publishing Ireland Limited,
29 Earlsfort Terrace, Dublin 2, D02 AY28, Ireland
1359 Broadway, 12th Floor, New York, NY 10018, USA
E-mail: info@ospreypublishing.com
www.ospreypublishing.com

OSPREY is a trademark of Osprey Publishing Ltd

First published in Great Britain in 2026

© Osprey Publishing Ltd, 2026

All rights reserved. No part of this publication may be: i) reproduced or transmitted in any form, electronic or mechanical, including photocopying, recording or by means of any information storage or retrieval system without prior permission in writing from the publishers; or ii) used or reproduced in any way for the training, development or operation of artificial intelligence (AI) technologies, including generative AI technologies. The rights holders expressly reserve this publication from the text and data mining exception as per Article 4(3) of the Digital Single Market Directive (EU) 2019/790

A catalogue record for this book is available from the British Library.

ISBN: PB 9781472872517; eBook 9781472872531; ePDF 9781472872500; XML 9781472872524

26 27 28 29 30 10 9 8 7 6 5 4 3 2 1

Maps by bounford.com
Diagrams by Adam Tooby
Index by Richard Munro
Typeset by Lumina Datamatics Ltd
Printed by Repro India Ltd.

Osprey Publishing supports the Woodland Trust, the UK's leading woodland conservation charity.

To find out more about our authors and books visit www.ospreypublishing.com. Here you will find extracts, author interviews, details of forthcoming events and the option to sign up for our newsletter.

For product safety related questions contact productsafety@bloomsbury.com

CONTENTS

THE FLEET'S PURPOSE

INTRODUCTION

Although it had been discussed for long enough, it took the Allies until the twin disasters of Pearl Harbor and the invasion of Malaya to create ABDA. In a conference held in Washington DC in late December 1941, a joint American, British, Dutch and Australian (ABDA) military command was proposed, to coordinate the response to the tide of Japanese offensive operations in South-East Asia. On 1 January 1942, ABDA Command (or ABDA COM) came into being, under the command of the British desert veteran Gen. Sir Archibald Wavell. His area of responsibility extended from the border with Burma in the west to New Guinea and the north-western coast of Australia to the east and south. In the north, it officially reached as far as Hong Kong and Formosa, although in practice these were already under Japanese control. The Philippines, governed by the USA, remained semi-independent, under the command of Gen. MacArthur.

The climax of the Battle of the Java Sea showing ABDA light cruisers trying to evade a spread of Japanese Type 93 torpedoes, 26 February 1942. In the foreground are HNLMS *Java* (left) and HMAS *Perth* (right), while behind them HNLMS *De Ruyter* has already been torpedoed, and is on fire and sinking. (Artwork by John Hamilton. Copy of original in the US Navy Art Collection)

This was an immense area, some 3,200 by 2,600 miles across (or 2,750 × 2,300nm). When ABDA was created, much of this territory was already under attack or had been conquered, including Malaya, Indochina, Borneo and the Philippines. Just as worryingly, the military and naval resources available to Wavell were pitifully small and outdated, compared to those available to the powerful Japanese forces allocated for the conquest of South-East Asia. ABDA's naval commander, Adm. Hart USN, was given the task of defending the grandly named 'Malay Barrier' – the semi-circular line from Malaya and Sumatra eastwards to Timor. This was ABDA's naval 'stop line' – the defence of which would ensure freedom of movement in the Indian Ocean, and between the East Indies and Australia, and ultimately to and from both Britain and the United States.

The naval threat couldn't have been greater. The Japanese conquest of the Philippines continued apace and led to the loss of much of the US Navy's Asiatic Fleet. The fall of Singapore on 15 February rendered the Malay Barrier indefensible, and a succession of Japanese assaults saw the steady erosion of ABDA territory throughout the East Indies. Ten days after Singapore fell, Wavell resigned his command, handing over control of ABDA to local commanders. Hart had also been replaced, at a time when unit of command might have salvaged something from the approaching disaster. So, it was left to a Dutch commander, R. Adm. Doorman, to lead ABDA's naval strike force into battle.

While ABDA enjoyed a minor success off Balikpapan in Borneo in late January, only the most naïve optimist could see anything other than disaster in what lay ahead. This book traces the challenges facing the commanders of ABDA, and their ships and men in this forlorn attempt to halt the Japanese juggernaut. It is a story which incorporates accounts of missed opportunities and major blunders, but also tells of moments of great heroism and sacrifice in the face of overwhelming odds. Crucially, the lessons learned from this example of international wartime cooperation in the face of a common threat are every bit as apt today as they were in World War II.

Northampton-class heavy cruiser USS *Houston* was the most powerful warship in ABDA, boasting nine 8in guns in three triple turrets, although like all of her kind the cruiser was relatively lightly protected. During the campaign, *Houston* earned the nickname 'Galloping Ghost of the Java Coast'.

FLEET FIGHTING POWER

ABDA STRIKING FORCE

To those who studied current affairs, the signs were there that Japan was on course for a war with the Western Powers who had a stake in the Pacific. The nation with the largest commitment there was the United States of America, but Great Britain, France and the Netherlands also maintained colonies in South-East Asia. While the increasingly militaristic stance of Japan and the dramatic expansion of the Imperial Japanese Navy during the decade before 1941 set alarm bells ringing in diplomatic and military circles, none of these powers did much to counter this growing threat. In early December 1941 they paid the price.

In 1914, Japan sided with the Allies in World War I, and as a result gained control of a number of German colonies in the Pacific. A few years before, Japan had annexed the Chinese island of Formosa, and then Korea. This though, was only the start of the Japanese land grab. In September 1931, the 'Manchurian Incident', a false-flag bomb attack on a Japanese-owned railway in Manchuria, led to the Japanese invasion of this sprawling Chinese province. International condemnation led to Japan's withdrawal, but the seeds were set for further confrontation between an increasingly militaristic Japan and a China wracked by civil war. In 1933, Japan left the League of Nations, and two years later it withdrew from the London Naval Conference, which was attempting to reduce naval expansion.

After that, the Japanese embarked on an ambitious five-year programme which saw their navy almost double in size. During the same period the United States, Britain and its Commonwealth and the Netherlands built very little in comparison. It was only when the likelihood of war became clearly evident that they set aside frugality, and began laying down much-needed new warships, or modernized their existing fleets. In July 1937, the 'Marco Polo Bridge Incident' led directly to war between Japan and China. This engineered affair at Wanping near Peking (now Beijing) gave the Japanese an excuse to invade, and soon Shanghai, Nanking (now Nanjun) and Wuhan were in Japanese hands. So too was much of northern China and key points along its coast. International attempts to broker a peace were rejected, and so in mid-1940 the United States imposed sanctions on Japan, and in July 1941 froze Japanese and Chinese assets in America, in an attempt to force both sides to the negotiating table. Instead, it set Japan on a course which would lead directly to Pearl Harbor.

Schout-bij-Nacht (R. Adm.) Karel Doorman RNN, commander of ABDA's Combined Striking Force. Although undoubtedly able and courageous, Doorman lacked the experience needed to take on the Japanese Navy, especially given the very limited tactical options available to him.

Meanwhile, the outbreak of war in Europe in September 1939 had presented further opportunities to the Japanese military leadership. Japan though, remained neutral and waited to see if the conflict might present it with further opportunities for expansion. In the summer of 1940, the fall of France and the Netherlands meant their colonial possessions in South-East Asia could no longer rely on assistance from Europe. To stave off invasion, the Japanese were granted military access to French Indochina, in return for recognition of Vichy France's sovereignty over the colony. However, this led to what amounted to the Japanese military occupation of French Indochina, albeit one where the existing Vichy French government of the colony remained in place. This military occupation though, gave the Japanese a useful springboard for further conquests in the region.

In early September 1941 an Imperial Conference in the presence of the Emperor Hirohito agreed that if diplomatic counter-demands weren't met, Japan would go to war with the United States, as well as Britain and the Netherlands. By November, detailed plans developed by Adm. Yamamoto, and Gen. Terauchi had been prepared for the Japanese conquest of the Philippines, the Dutch East Indies, and the British territories of Malaya, Hong Kong and Singapore. V. Adm. Nagumo was also issued his orders to carry out a pre-emptive strike on the US Naval base at Pearl Harbor in Hawaii. When the US rejected Japan's demands and stuck by their own insistence that the Japanese withdraw from China and newly occupied Indonesia, the chance of a peaceful solution passed.

The Whirlwind

On 27 November, Nagumo's Striking Force put to sea, bound for Hawaii. In Formosa, the Japanese 14th Army and the Third Fleet prepared to launch the invasion of the Philippines, while V. Adm. Ozawa's Expeditionary Force was already at Cam Ranh Bay in Indochina, ready to carry out its planned landings on Malaya's eastern coast. On 2 December, a signal was sent to all Japanese naval units, confirming that 'X-Day' – the start of these attacks – would be 8 December (or 7 December in Hawaii, on the far side of the International Date Line). By 27 November Adm. Stark, the US Chief of Naval Operations, issued a 'War Warning', and told Adm. Hart, commanding the US Asiatic Fleet in the Philippines, that conflict was imminent. However, with his limited forces, there was little that Hart could do, apart from put his ships on alert, and hope Stark was wrong.

While an attack on the Philippines was expected, few realized that Japan's opening gambit would be an attack on Pearl Harbor. The Japanese Carrier Strike Force reached its launch position 275 miles north of Pearl Harbor at 0600hrs on 7 December. The initial air attack reached its target – the anchored US Pacific Fleet – at 0755hrs, and the attack began immediately, as the anchored ships were about to commence the morning colours ceremony at 0800hrs. The attack was a success – at 0810hrs the battleship USS *Arizona* exploded in a fireball, and 1,100 American sailors were killed. Other ships suffered too. By the time the attackers withdrew, four battleships had been sunk, and four others were damaged, as were several other smaller warships. The raid also targeted airfields, destroying 188 American aircraft on the ground. Of the death toll of 2,043, almost half perished aboard the *Arizona*. From the Japanese standpoint, the attack on Pearl Harbor was a great success, achieved at the minimal cost of 29 aircraft. However, V. Adm. Nagumo, who led the Japanese Carrier Strike Force, noted that no American carriers were in Pearl Harbor that morning. The Japanese commander knew that in the conflict which would inevitably follow, their existence was more important than a squadron of battleships.

The old American light cruiser USS *Marblehead* pictured entering New York harbour in late 1942. The ship was damaged in an air attack in the Flores Sea on 4 February, and after temporary repairs in Tjilatjap in Java, *Marblehead* was sent to Ceylon and then to the United States for repairs.

The first wave's attack at 0755hrs on Sunday 7 December was in Hawaii time. However, confusingly, 4,600nm to the east, on the opposite side of the International Date Line, it was 18½ hours later (it has since been re-adjusted to 18 hours). This meant that when the Pearl Harbor attack began, in Cavite, home of the US Asiatic Fleet outside Manila in the Philippines, it was 0225hrs on Monday 8 December. News of the attack reached the Philippines within minutes, but Gen. MacArthur, in charge of the archipelago's defence, sought confirmation from Washington DC before initiating his pre-arranged war plans. At 1240hrs, Japanese aircraft operating from Formosa bombed Clark Field to the north of Manila, destroying around 100 American aircraft. A little earlier, carrier-based aircraft had also attacked targets in the Philippines main island, Luzon – a sure sign that a Japanese task force was in the area. So, belatedly, the US Asiatic Fleet was ordered to prepared for action.

Meanwhile, in Singapore the British were also preparing to confront the Japanese. On 2 December, 'Force G' arrived in Singapore. Commanded by Adm. Tom Phillips, it consisted of the battleship HMS *Prince of Wales* and the battlecruiser HMS *Repulse*. Phillips flew to the Philippines to consult with Hart, but returned to Singapore on 6 December when a Japanese invasion fleet was sighted heading for the eastern coast of Malaya. Hart was sending four US destroyers to Singapore, and Phillips recalled the three British destroyers at Hong Kong, ordering them to Singapore as well.

Early on Monday 8 December, word came of Japanese landings at Kota Bharu, 400 miles to the north, near the Siam–Malaya border. Then, reports came in of Japanese attacks on Pearl Harbor, Hong Kong and the Philippines. Singapore was also subjected to a light raid. Phillips decided to put to sea, rather than risk an air attack in harbour. There, he'd be in a position to attack the Japanese landing force. So, at 1710hrs, *Prince of Wales* and *Repulse* left Singapore, accompanied by four destroyers. Phillip's force was also redesignated 'Force Z'.

Low cloud and rain cloaked Force Z as it headed into the Gulf of Siam, but the next afternoon it was spotted by a Japanese submarine. Other Japanese sightings followed. By dawn (0503hrs) on Wednesday 10 December, Force Z was 50 miles off the coast, near Kuantan, investigating reports of a Japanese landing there. After discovering this was a Japanese diversionary ruse, Phillips turned away from the coast again and steamed south-east, waiting for land-based air cover that arrived minutes too late.

By then the Japanese had a good idea of where Force Z was. At dawn, nine search aircraft left Saigon, followed 90 minutes later by three waves of land-based naval strike aircraft – a total of 83 bombers and torpedo planes. At 1015hrs, Force Z was spotted, and the bombers were directed towards the British force. At 1113hrs, Force Z was subjected to the first of several air attacks. *Repulse* was hit by a 250kg bomb, suffering minor damage, but almost 30 minutes later a wave of torpedo-bombers carried out another attack, and

Prince of Wales was hit by two torpedoes. One of these struck the battleship on her port quarter, buckling a propeller shaft. This caused a heavy list and reduced the speed of Phillip's flagship to 15kts, rendering her unable to evade further attacks. In contrast, *Repulse* evaded all of the torpedoes launched at the battlecruiser.

By noon, it was clear *Prince of Wales* was in trouble, so Phillips contacted Singapore, demanding air cover. Instead, at 1221hrs, the third Japanese wave appeared, and two minutes later the battleship was hit by three torpedoes on the starboard side. *Repulse* was attacked from multiple directions and was hit by five torpedoes. With his ship sinking, Capt. Tennant gave the order to abandon ship. At 1241hrs, it was the turn of *Prince of Wales*, as a fresh Japanese strike wave appeared. This time the battleship was hit by a 500kg bomb amidships, causing extensive damage. It was clear that *Prince of Wales* was sinking, and so at 1310hrs, 40 minutes after *Repulse* sank, Capt. Leach ordered his crew to abandon ship. *Prince of Wales* finally capsized and sank at 1323hrs, minutes after the long-awaited fighter cover finally arrived.

The loss of the two Royal Navy capital ships was something of a seismic shift in naval history. It was a clear demonstration that the days of the battleship were over. From that point on, naval airpower was the most effective asset in the naval arsenal. In Singapore it had a more immediate effect. It stripped Malaya of any naval protection and demonstrated that the Japanese rather than the British had control of the Gulf of Siam. Consequently, the buildup of the Japanese bridgehead continued uninterrupted. After securing both sides of the Malay peninsula the Japanese advanced through Malaya, driving the British and Commonwealth forces there back towards Singapore. The limited air assets available to the defenders were hopelessly outnumbered and could do nothing to turn the tide. By the New Year of 1942, it was clear that the Japanese were going to conquer Malaya. That meant the fate of Singapore also hung in the balance.

The Allied Reaction

It was clear that the United States and Great Britain were facing a common threat, and shortly the Dutch colonies in the East Indies would be confronted with it too. However, despite meetings and vague rhetoric about combining against a common enemy, no workable joint command was established before the war began. So, for the moment, despite unofficial support from the others, it was every nation for itself. On 10 December, the US Naval base at Cavite near Manila was bombed, destroying much of the base's infrastructure. By then though, only obsolete or inactive warships remained. Adm. Hart had already taken the bulk of his operational force to sea. On 12 December, with the approval of his superiors, Hart withdrew the majority of the US Asiatic Fleet to Java in the Dutch East Indies, where for the time being it would be safe from air attack.

The meeting of the senior officers of ABDA Striking Force in Sourabaya in the early evening of 26 February – the eve of the sortie that led to the Battle of the Java Sea. At the head of the table is R. Adm. Doorman, the Dutch commander of the force, addressing his captains and staff officers. Within just over 24 hours, Doorman and several of these officers would be dead.

That same day, 12 December, the first Japanese landings took place near Legazpi in southern Luzon. Other landings followed in the north of the island, and the Japanese began their advance through Luzon towards Manila, heading from both the north and the south-east of the island. MacArthur's outnumbered and outclassed defenders did what they could to stem the Japanese advance, but they were steadily pushed back. By then of course, the only naval support left was the US Asiatic Fleet's submarine force, which remained in Philippine waters – the boats submerging during the day to avoid detection, and refuelling and rearming under cover of darkness. MacArthur would later criticize Hart for the inability of these submarines to prevent the Japanese from landing. In fact they tried, but faulty torpedoes rendered their efforts less effective than had been expected.

Once the Japanese army began its steady advance on Manila, the fate of the Philippine capital was even more precarious than that of Singapore. So, on 24 December Hart issued orders for his defenders to withdraw to a defensive perimeter at Bataan, a rugged volcanic peninsula 20 miles away from the capital, on the far side of Manila Bay. There, the Americans and Filipino defenders would hold out, hoping against hope that relief would come.

MacArthur hope that relief would come. Meanwhile, in Washington and London, President Roosevelt and Prime Minister Churchill were wrestling with the notion of a joint Allied command in the region. They agreed one should be established, and selected Gen. Wavell to command it. The reluctance to name an American commander might well have been political, as there was a general assumption that the challenge of defending the region had become a lost cause. So, Wavell became the commander of all land, sea and air forces in the theatre, which was dubbed the American, British, Dutch and Australian Command – or ABDA COM for short. It was finally activated on 15 January 1942.

Adm. Phillips had been lost with his flagship *Prince of Wales*, so the thankless task of commanding ABDA's remaining naval assets was given to the most senior naval officer in the theatre, Adm. Hart, who duly became ABDA Float. However, as the Royal Dutch Navy made up the largest portion of the force, command of the ABDA Combined Striking Force was given to a Dutchman, R. Adm. Doorman. Another needless administrative layer was also imposed, with British, American and Dutch naval commanders in charge of their own nation's force. It was an unwieldy arrangement, but it was forged quickly, and in the heat of battle, so in time the structure could be revised and improved. Unfortunately for ABDA, time wasn't a quantity that was readily available.

THE SHIPS

Pre-war preparations by the Americans, British and Dutch in South-East Asia had been minimal. Obviously, the Dutch could expect no help from the German-occupied Netherlands, and so they had to make do with the very limited resources they had to hand. For their part, by December 1941 the British had been at war for over two years, and the Royal Navy had been heavily committed in home waters and the Mediterranean. Despite a string of naval successes, losses had been heavy, particularly in the Mediterranean. This, combined with the need to repair damaged or worn-out ships and machinery meant that there was little appetite at the Admiralty to commit much-needed warships to the Far East. Still, new fleet carriers and battleships were entering service, and Churchill was adamant that some of these would be sent to reinforce the scant Royal Navy force stationed at Singapore. Reluctantly, the First Sea Lord, Adm. Sir Dudley Pound,

HMS *Exeter*, one of two York-class heavy cruisers, rose to prominence in December 1939 thanks to the ship's key part in the Battle of the River Plate. Over two years later, *Exeter* was the largest warship in the Royal Navy's contingent serving with ABDA. However, with only six 8in guns, *Exeter* was no match for the ship's larger and better-armed Japanese counterparts.

agreed to send the new battleship HMS *Prince of Wales* and the battlecruiser HMS *Repulse* there, accompanied by the new fleet carrier HMS *Indomitable*. These were due to arrive there in early December. It really was a case of too little, too late, particularly as thanks to a grounding, the carrier never reached Singapore.

It was a similar situation with the US Asiatic Fleet, based in the Philippines. The US Navy's standing naval force in the western Pacific was woefully inadequate. It consisted of three cruisers, one of which was modern, and a flotilla of largely obsolete destroyers, as well as a number of lesser vessels, such as gunboats and support vessels. The most effective element of the fleet was its sizeable submarine force. However, in the event of a war, the Asiatic Fleet would be hard-pressed to achieve much in the face of a full-scale Japanese offensive.

Even with this fresh British commitment, the naval balance in South-East Asia was skewed heavily in favour of the Japanese. On the eve of war, the following warships were available for immediate service in South-East Asia:

AVAILABLE WARSHIPS (7 DECEMBER 1941)

	Royal Navy's Eastern Fleet	Royal Navy's East Indies Squadron	Anzac Squadrons	Royal Netherlands Navy East Indies Force	US Asiatic Fleet	Total available
Aircraft Carriers	-	(1)		-	-	-
Battleships & Battlecruisers	2	1*		-	-	**2**
Cruisers	3	1 (2)	5	3 (1)	3	**15**
Destroyers	5 (6)		2 (2)	7	11 (2)	**25**
Submarines	1			13 (1)	25 (4)	**39**

* The battleship *Revenge* was based in Ceylon, but Admiralty orders limited the ship's deployment further east than the Indian Ocean. The numbers in brackets represent additional warships which were undergoing refits and so were non-operational. The Royal Navy's total includes two destroyers (*Scout* and *Thanet*) stationed in Hong Kong. Also in the colony was a flotilla of eight Motor Torpedo Boats (MTBs).

The only other modern surface ship in the US Navy's ABDA contingent was USS *Boise*, a Brooklyn-class light cruiser. However, *Boise* only played a limited part in the campaign, having been damaged while striking an uncharted shoal in the Sape Strait on 22 January. The cruiser was then sent to Bombay for temporary repairs.

The Royal Navy's East Indies Squadron is included, although apart from the heavy cruiser HMS *Exeter*, which was en route to Singapore when the Japanese launched their offensive, the squadron was based in Ceylon (now Sri Lanka) and the elderly battleship HMS *Revenge* was under orders to protect shipping in the Indian Ocean. So, only *Exeter* is included in the total of Allied warships available for immediate service. This list takes no account of the numerous lesser warships such as sloops, gunboats or armed merchant cruisers, which were of little military value.

By contrast, V. Adm. Kondo's Southern Force had the following Japanese warships poised to commence operations in South-East Asian waters:

AVAILABLE SHIPS: IJN SOUTHERN FORCE				
	Philippines Invasion Group (V. Adm. Takahashi)	**Malaya Invasion Group (V. Adm. Ozawa)**	**Distant Cover Group (V. Adm. Kondo)**	**Total available**
Aircraft Carriers	1+2	-	-	**3**
Battleships & Battlecruisers	-	-	2	**2**
Cruisers	10	7	4	**21**
Destroyers	30	14	10	**54**
Submarines	-	-	18	**18**

The listing of aircraft carriers comprises the light carrier IJNS *Ryujo*, with 34 aircraft embarked, while the two listed after the plus sign are the Seaplane Carriers IJNS *Chitose* and IJNS *Mizuho*, each with 20 seaplanes embarked.

Again, this total takes no account of smaller vessels, such as patrol craft, minesweepers or support vessels. Not listed, but of some relevance here, is the Hong Kong Bombardment Unit, detached from the Second Fleet, consisting of a light cruiser (IJNS *Isuzu*) and three destroyers.

This shows that the Japanese enjoyed a significant numerical advantage. This is without even considering the land-based naval aircraft available to V. Adm. Kondo. Of course, it wasn't just a matter of numbers. For the most part, the ships of the Japanese Second and Third Fleets that took part in operations in the theatre were modern, state-of-the-art warships. In theory the Second Fleet based on Hainan had 11 modern heavy cruisers with 8in guns at its disposal, while the Third Fleet based on Formosa had one heavy cruiser, supported by a few older light cruisers.

Each fleet also used light cruisers as destroyer flotilla leaders, while the numerous destroyers they led were all modern, fast ships. This doesn't even consider the superiority of the Japanese Type 93 'Long Lance' torpedo. Its range would come as a nasty shock to ABDA Command's Striking Force. Two Kongo-class fast battleships (IJNS *Kongo* and IJNS *Haruna*) were also deployed in reserve, as part of Adm. Kondo's Distant Cover Force. Now that

Force Z had been destroyed, ABDA Float had nothing that could match their firepower. As the campaign progressed, other warships were made available from the overall command – the Combined Fleet – particularly those that had participated in the Pearl Harbor operation.

The Australian light cruiser HMAS *Hobart* was a sister-ship of HMAS *Perth*. Both were modified Leander-class light cruisers, but only *Hobart* survived the campaign. For the most part, the cruiser was deployed on convoy protection duties in the Indian Ocean, but in late February *Hobart* briefly formed part of the Western Striking Force, before being withdrawn from the theatre.

Put simply, the Allied warships deployed in defence of the Malay Barrier and the East Indies weren't really up to the task. Setting aside the Royal Navy, which had been hardened on the anvil of war, both the US Pacific Fleet and the Royal Dutch Navy weren't trained to the peak wartime proficiency of their opponents, and they paid the price. The Japanese ships were also, for the most part, much more powerful than those available to ABDA Float. Save *Exeter* and the USS *Houston*, the only 8in cruisers available to it, its small cruiser force was made up of 6in cruisers, which would be considerably outgunned by their 8in rivals. The Japanese were also supported by a substantial land-based air arm and even had their own light aircraft carrier in the area. By contrast the Allies lacked adequate fighter protection or reconnaissance aircraft, as US losses in the Philippines and British ones in Malaya had greatly depleted the pool of available aircraft.

The Royal Navy and Australian Navy's forces deployed in ABDA Float were of decidedly limited effectiveness. *Exeter*, the only British heavy cruiser, carried just six 8in guns, which compared poorly with a typical Japanese counterpart, the IJNS *Nachi*, which mounted ten 8in guns. Although *Exeter* was the only ship in ABDA that carried an air warning radar. All British-built cruisers were more lightly armoured than most of the Japanese ones, and the D-class cruisers in Singapore were regarded as obsolete and unsuited to front-line service. That left HMAS *Perth*, with eight 6in guns to counter Japan's heavy cruisers.

As for British-built destroyers, these were a mixed lot, with *Electra*, *Encounter*, *Express* and *Jupiter* being modern, with veteran crews, but still smaller and less well-armed than their Japanese counterparts. The older S-class destroyers in the theatre were built soon after World War I and were even less well-armed than the other British destroyers serving in ABDA. So, like the D-class cruisers, they took no significant part in the campaign.

The US Asiatic Fleet was considered expendable in wartime, and this reflected its composition. The exception were two modern cruisers, the Washington Treaty-era Northampton-class heavy cruiser USS *Houston*, with nine 8in guns and the Brooklyn-class light cruiser USS *Boise*, which carried 15 6in guns. Both would be useful assets to any navy. These cruisers had a reasonably strong

When HMAS *Perth* returned to Australia from the Mediterranean, the plain light grey scheme shown here had been replaced by a splinter-grey camouflage pattern of light and dark grey, although there is evidence the port side had been overpainted before the Battle of the Java Sea. *Perth* was sunk on 1 March in the Battle of the Sunda Strait.

anti-aircraft (AA) battery, with *Houston* mounting eight 5in AA guns. The fleet's third cruiser, USS *Marblehead*, was much older though, having been commissioned in 1924, and by 1941 was considered unsuitable for front-line duties, much like the even older British D-class light cruisers based in Singapore.

As for the Asiatic Fleet's destroyers, they were all of the Clemson class, built during the US Navy's expansion from 1917, most having entered service soon after the end of World War I. By 1941 they were obsolete and armed with a weak battery of single 4in mounts, bolstered by torpedo tubes and a token AA battery. They were hard pressed to make 30kts, and many were suffering from serious maintenance problems. The jewel in the Asiatic Fleet's crown was really its force of fleet submarines – most of which were modern Porpoise-, Sargo- and Salmon-class boats. These though, before the creation of ABDA, would suffer a severe setback when their base at Cavite was bombed on 10 December. At a stroke, most of their stock of torpedoes and stores were lost, together with the communication centre, which had been purpose built to control the boats when they were at sea.

Before the war, the Royal Netherlands Navy had maintained an East Indies Squadron, which was primarily based at Sourabaya (now Surabaya) on the north coast of Java. In 1941 the fall of the Netherlands in May 1940 had deprived the squadron of any support from home, and it was largely left to its own devices. Still, it was a reasonably powerful force – at least by peacetime standards. It consisted of three light cruisers (HNLMS *De Ruyter*, HNLMS *Java* and HNLMS *Tromp*). Despite being commissioned in the 1930s, they were all essentially slightly modernized versions of World War I designs. *De Ruyter*, flagship of the squadron, mounted seven 6in guns, all but one of which were in twin turrets, while the two smaller Tromp-class cruisers carried six guns, all in twin turrets, as well as torpedoes, which *De Ruyter* lacked. However, the flagship, being slightly larger, had space for a pair of float planes.

They were supported by a small flotilla of Admirals-class destroyers, in two sub-classes, all of which entered service in the late 1920s. They were designed by the British firm of Yarrow and so resembled British medium destroyers of the same generation. All were armed with four 12cm (4.7in) guns, and six torpedo tubes, mounting British-built torpedoes. The second batch – the Van Gelen class – had a slightly improved AA armament, which included a 40mm Bofors gun, as well as a 3in AA gun and machine guns. Finally, the Dutch had a surprisingly sizeable force of 15 submarines stationed in the East Indies. Although most of these were of dated 1920s designs, they proved reasonably effective during the campaign. The real problem facing the Dutch squadron was its lack of support from home, owing to the occupation of the Netherlands, which meant the lack of manpower and spare parts reduced the effectiveness of their warships.

During the air attack on Darwin on 19 February, the destroyer USS *Peary* got under way, in an attempt to evade the Japanese bombers. However, at 1010hrs while still in Darwin Roads, *Peary* was hit by five bombs and set ablaze. The final bomb broke the old destroyer's keel, and *Peary* sank quickly, with the loss of 80 crew.

Taken as a whole, even a soldier like Gen. Wavell, the ABDA Commander-in-Chief, couldn't help but notice the limitations of ABDA's naval arm. Three different navies – or four if you separated the Royal Australian Navy's contingent from the Royal Navy's one – meant supply problems, because of different needs, types and calibres of weaponry and mechanical condition. There wasn't much of a language problem, as the majority of Dutch officers could communicate well enough in English. More of an issue was the way the various navies went about their business. Each had their own tactical doctrine, based around their equipment, and their perceived duty. The same was true of administrative procedures, or the way the various warships were run.

Morale was an issue too. In the Dutch Navy, morale was surprisingly high, as the Dutch crews were all fighting for their own territory. Many of the crewmen had been recruited in the East Indies, and had family ties there, or had been stationed there long enough to have brought out their families. The British and Australian crews had all, for the most part, seen action before, in the Mediterranean or the Atlantic. After two years of war, their ships' companies had had time to weld themselves into efficient and professional fighting formations. However, morale had suffered a knock following the sinking of Force Z, and inevitably there was apprehension that the same fate might befall them. Still, they had faith in their ship and their shipmates and could be counted on when the need arose.

Morale among the sailors of the US Asiatic Fleet was less easy to calculate. For almost all of them this was their first taste of war, and it was a particularly gruelling introduction to it. Any outrage following the attack on Pearl Harbor might have been replaced by a need for revenge, but for many the bombing of their own base at Cavite on 10 December was a salutary experience, which gave them pause for thought. It was later claimed that many American seamen resented being called upon to what – as they saw it – was the protection of colonial powers such as Britain and the Netherlands.

Of course, the United States was no stranger to colonialism, but these were foreign colonial systems, which somehow made a difference. Morale also suffered during the campaign, as the crews felt they had been abandoned by the rest of the navy. In general though, lack of wartime experience was overcome by training, but even here the Asiatic Fleet had been lax, and so the crews would have to learn wartime proficiency the hard way – in action.

These though, were all problems which, in theory, were surmountable, or at least would be if ABDA Float had the time it needed to overcome them. Unfortunately, it didn't. Instead, it was immediately pitched straight into the crucible of war. The biggest hurdle, of course, was the fighting potential of ABDA, compared to that of the enemy. The combined American, British, Dutch and Australian force was made up of largely obsolete warships, which were poorly suited to the needs of modern naval combat.

This, however, might have been less of a concern if ABDA and the enemy it faced were more evenly matched. Unfortunately, V. Adm. Kondo's Southern Force was both larger and more powerful. Kondo's naval assets included a pair of battleships, numerous modern and well-armed heavy cruisers and several squadrons of large, modern destroyers. Put simply, ABDA was both outnumbered and outgunned. Nevertheless, Adm. Hart and his men would simply have to make the best of this distinctly unpromising situation and do what they could to stem the Japanese tide.

ABDA NAVAL FORCES: 15 JANUARY 1942

Royal Naval Contingent

Heavy Cruiser (one vessel)	Modified York class	*Exeter* (Capt. Gordon)	
Light Cruisers (six vessels)	Perth Class (Royal Australian Navy)	*Hobart* (Capt. Howden)	
		Perth (Capt. Waller)	
	D class	*Dragon* (Capt. Shaw)	
		Danae (Capt. Butler)	
		Durban (Capt. Cazalet)	
		Dauntless (Capt. Hewitt)	
Destroyers (8)	E class	*Electra* (H27) (Cdr May)	Sunk 27 February 1942
		Encounter (H10) (Lt Cdr St J. Morgan)	Sunk 1 March 1942
		Express (H61) (Lt Cdr Cartwright)	Transferred to Canadian Navy 1943
	J, K and N class	*Jupiter* (F85) (Lt Cdr Thew)	Sunk 27 February 1942
	Admiralty S class	*Scout* (H51) (Lt Cdr Lambton)	Broken up 1946
		Stronghold (H50) (Lt Cdr Pretor-Pinney)	Sunk 2 March 1942
		Tenedos (H04) (Lt Dyer)	Sunk 5 April 1942
		Thanet (H29) (Cdr Davies)	Sunk 27 January 1942

Royal Netherlands Naval Contingent

Light cruisers (three vessels)	De Ruyter class	*De Ruyter* (Capt. Lacomblé)	Sunk 28 February 1942
	Sumatra class	*Java* (Capt. van Straelen)	Sunk 27 February 1942
	Tromp class	*Tromp* (Capt. de Meester)	Broken up 1958
Destroyers (seven vessels)	Admirals class (1st Group) or Van Ghent class	*Evertsen* (Lt Cdr de Vries)	Lost 29 February 1942
		Kortenaer (Lt Cdr Kroese)	Sunk 27 February 1942
		Van Ghent (Lt Cdr Shotel)	Wrecked 15 February 1942
		Piet Hein (Lt Cdr Chömpff)	Sunk 19 February 1942
	Admirals class (2nd Group) or Van Galen class	*Banckert* (Lt Cdr Goslings)	Sunk as target ship September 1949
		Van Nes (Lt Cdr Lagaay)	Scuttled 2 March 1942
		Witte de With (Lt Cdr Shotel)	Scuttled 2 March 1942

Minesweepers (two vessels)	Lapwing class (Attached from US Navy)	*Lark* (AM-21) (Lt Cdr Thomson)	Broken up 1947
		Whipporwhill (AM-35) (Lt Cdr Ferriter)	Broken up 1946
Submarines (15 boats)	KV class	*K-7*	(*K-7* sunk 18 February 1942)
	KVIII class	*K-8, K-9, K-10*	
	KXI class	*K-11, K-12, K-13*	(*K-13* sunk 2 March 1942)
	KIV class	*K-14, K-15, K-16*	(*K-16* sunk 25 December 1941)
		K-17, K-18	(*K-17* lost late December 1941, *K-18* scuttled 2 March 1942)
	O-16 class	*O-16*	(*O-16* sunk 15 December 1941)
	O-19 class	*O-19, O-20*	(*O-19* scuttled 10 July 1945, *O-20* scuttled 19 December 1945)
All surviving boats decommissioned and broken up, 1942–46			

US Naval Contingent

Heavy cruiser (one vessel)	Northampton class	*Houston* (CA30) (Capt. Rooks)	
Light cruisers (two vessels)	Brooklyn class	*Boise* (CL47) (Capt. S.B. Robinson)	Sold 1951
	Marblehead class	*Marblehead* (CL12) (Capt. A.G. Robinson)	Broken up 1946
Destroyers (13 vessels) All Clemson class	Destroyer Squadron 29 (Capt. Wiley)	*Paul Jones* (DD230) (Lt Cdr Hourihan)	Broken up 1947
	Destroyer Division 57 (Cdr Crouch)	*Whipple* (DD217) (Lt Cdr Karpe)	Broken up 1946
		Alden (DD12) (Lt Cdr Coley)	Broken up 1945
		John D. Edwards (DD216) (Lt Cdr Eccles)	Broken up 1945
		Edsall (DD219) (Lt Cdr Nix)	Sunk 1942
	Destroyer Division 58 (Cdr Binford)	*Bulmer* (DD222) (Lt Cdr Manees) (Lt Cdr Harris after 28 January)	Broken up 1947
		Barker (DD213) (Lt Cdr Smith)	Broken up 1945
		Parrott (DD218) (Lt Cdr Parker) (Lt Cdr Hughes after 29 January)	Lost 1944
		Stewart (DD224) (Lt Cdr McGlone)	Lost 1942
	Destroyer Division 59 (Cdr Talbot – Lt Hughes from 29 January)	*Pope* (DD225) (Lt Cdr Blinn)	Lost 1942
		Peary (DD226) (Lt Cdr Bermingham)	Lost 1942
		Pillsbury (DD227) (Lt Cdr Pound)	Lost 1942
		John D. Ford (DD216) (Lt Cdr Cooper)	Broken up 1945
Submarines (29 vessels)	Task Force 3 (Capt. Wilkes)		
	Subron 20 (Base vessels)		
	Submarine tenders	USS *Holland* (AS-3) (Cdr Gregory)	
		USS *Canopus* (AS-9) (Cdr Sackett)	Scuttled off Bataan 9 April 1942
		USS *Otus* (AS-20) (Lt Cdr Newsom)	
	Submarine rescue ship	USS *Pigeon* (ASR-6) (Lt Cdr Davis)	Sunk off Corregidor 4 May 1942
	Submarine Division 21 (six boats)		
	Salmon class	*Salmon* (SS-182) (Lt McKinney)	
		Seal (SS-182) (Lt Cdr Hurd)	
		Skipjack (SS-183) (Lt Freeman)	
	Sargo class	*Sargo* (SS-188) (Lt Cdr Jacobs)	
		Saury (SS-189) (Lt Cdr Mewhinney)	
		Spearfish (SS-190) (Lt Price)	
	Submarine Division 22 (six boats)		
	Salmon class	*Snapper* (SS-185) (Lt Cdr Stone)	
		Stingray (SS-186) (Lt Cdr Moore)	
		Sturgeon (SS-187) (Lt Cdr Wright)	

	Sargo class	*Sculpin* (SS-191)	Sunk 19 November 1943
		Sailfish (SS-192) (Lt Cdr Voge (2nd command))	
		Swordfish (SS-193) (Lt Smith)	Sunk 12 January 1945
	Submarine Division 201 (six boats – all S class)		
		USS S-36 (SS-14) (Lt McKnight)	Wrecked and scuttled 21 January 1942
		USS S-37 (SS-142) (Lt Dempsey (Lt Reynolds from 26 February))	
		USS S-38 (SS-143) (Lt Chapple)	
		USS S-39 (SS-144) (Lt Coe)	Wrecked 14 August 1942
		USS S-40 (SS-145) (Lt Lucker)	
		USS S-41 (SS-146) (Lt Holley)	
	Submarine Division 202 (four boats)		
	Sargo class	USS *Seadragon* (SS-194) (Lt Cdr Ferrall)	
		USS *Searaven* (SS-196) (Lt Cdr Ayward)	
		USS *Seawolf* (SS-197) (Lt Cdr Warder)	Sunk 3 October 1944
	Balao class	USS *Sealion* (SS-195) (Lt Cdr Voge)	Scuttled 25 December 1942
	Submarine Division 202 (seven boats – all Porpoise class)		
		USS *Porpoise* (SS-172) (Lt Cdr Callaghan (Lt Cdr McKnight from 7 Feb))	
		USS *Pike* (SS-173) (Lt Cdr New)	
		USS *Shark* (SS-174) (Lt Cdr Shane)	Sunk 11 February 1942
		USS *Tarpon* (SS-175) (Lt Cdr Wallace)	
		USS *Perch* (SS-176) (Lt Cdr Hurt)	Sunk 3 March 1942
		USS *Pickerel* (SS-177) (Lt Cdr Bacon)	Lost April 1943
		USS *Permit* (SS-178) (Lt Cdr Hurst)	

TECHNOLOGY

Weaponry

The Washington Naval Treaty of February 1922 led naval construction in a new direction. Despite strict limitations on the number and displacement of fleets and warships, one loophole was the qualitative limit on cruiser construction, with a maximum displacement of 10,000 tons, carrying a main armament of 8in guns or less. This led the world's maritime powers to build a new class of 8in gun heavy cruisers. In the defence of the Malay Barrier in 1942, both ABDA Float and the Japanese Navy employed a number of these fairly powerful but relatively poorly protected warships – the Royal Navy's *Exeter*, the US Navy's *Houston* and the Japanese Navy's Nachi, Mogami and Takao classes. There was a difference between these. Owing to inter-war parsimony, *Exeter* only mounted six 8in guns, while *Houston*'s nine guns were comparable to the ten mounted in most of Japan's heavy cruisers.

These fired a 256–277lb (116–126kg) armour-piercing (AP) or high explosive (HE) shell, with a theoretical maximum range of 30,000–32,000yds (28,000–29,000m), but in practice effective range was more akin to 21,870yds

(21,000m). At that range, armour penetration was estimated at around 5in, and the rate of fire was around 4–5rpm. This all compared favourably with the 6in light cruisers in both ABDA Float and the Japanese Southern Group, with a typical maximum range of 25,000yds, and an effective one of around 14,000–16,000yds. These 112–130lb (52–59kg) 6in shells were also divided into AP and HE versions, with a rate of fire of 6–8rpm, with a penetration at effective range of 2–3in.

Again, there was a big difference between the armament of these light cruisers. Most of the Japanese and Dutch ones were similar to the American *Marblehead*, lacking a modern, effective fire control system, and in many cases guns in single inadequately protected mounts. However, *Boise* and the Australian *Perth* were more modern and were well served by modern fire control directors. The best of the light cruisers though, were the Japanese Mogami class, which mounted 15 guns in five triple turrets, guided by an effective modern gun director. Similarly, there was a significant difference between the quality of the rival destroyers in the campaign. The 4in/50 rapid-firing guns of the Asiatic Fleet's destroyers were of limited use, and lacked any effective director, and while the 4.7in weapons of the Dutch destroyers were slightly more modern, they too lacked a modern fire control system.

In fact, only the twin-mounted 4.7in guns of the two 'E- and F-' and one 'J-, K- and N-' class British destroyers and the even more modern Japanese Asashio-, Kagero- and Shiratsuyu-class destroyers with their twin-mounted 5in guns were well provided in terms of fire control systems. However, they all lacked the ability to act as truly effective high-angle AA guns, which meant the destroyers had to rely on their smaller close-range AA guns, and of course their speed and agility to protect themselves during air attacks. As for the cruisers, *Houston* mounted 5in high-angle AA guns, while *Exeter* and *Perth* carried 4in ones, supported by dedicated high-angle gun directors. Otherwise, ABDA's

USS *Langley* was the US Navy's first aircraft carrier, having entered service in 1922. In 1936–37 *Langley* was converted into a seaplane carrier, and by 1941 was serving with the US Asiatic Fleet, before being sent to Australia. On 22 February, *Langley* sailed from Darwin with 32 P-40 fighters embarked, bound for Java. The carrier though, was sunk 50 miles off Tjilatjap by Japanese Betty bombers operating from Bali.

cruisers and destroyers carried the standard AA defences of this stage of the war – single 3in AA mountings, multiple machine-gun mounts and 2pdr (40mm) 'pom-poms'. However, the Dutch cruisers also had the more effective 40mm Hazemeyer automatic AA guns, a precursor of the 40mm Bofors gun, which was supported by its own gun director.

All of the destroyers and submarines in ABDA as well as most of the cruisers carried 21in (53.3cm) torpedoes. Among the cruisers, *Northampton* had six tubes in two triple launchers, as did *Exeter*, while the three Perth-class light cruisers carried eight in two quadruple launchers, and *Marblehead* had four in two twins. *Boise*, *De Ruyter* and *Java* didn't mount any torpedoes, but *Tromp* did, in two triple mountings. As for the destroyers, the two British E and F class mounted eight in two quadruple launchers, while *Javelin* carried ten in two quintuple ones. The Dutch had six in two triples, while most of the Clemson-class destroyers of the US Asiatic fleet had 12 torpedoes in four triple launchers. Some though, had been modified, and two launchers had been removed to make way for a 3in AA gun. The same weapon was used in British or Dutch submarines.

Both the Australians, the British and the Dutch used the British 21in Mark VIII torpedo, which was first introduced in 1927, and had been modified slightly by 1941–42. It had a range of up to 7,000yds at 41kts, or 5,000yds at 45½kts, and packed an explosive charge of 722lb (327kg of TNT). By this stage, an improved version using the more powerful Torpex explosive was available and used in most Australian or British warships. However, the Dutch still used TNT for their explosive charge. The US Navy also used 21in torpedoes, with the Mark 14 carried in its submarines and the Mark 15 in cruisers. The latter had a range of 14,000yds at 26½kts, 9,000yds at 33½kts or 4,500yds at 45kts. The Asiatic Fleet's destroyers though, mounted the Mark 8 torpedo, first introduced in 1915, which had a theoretical maximum range of 16,000yds. In fact 10,000yds at 27kts was the norm in 1941–42. However, it was prone

BATTLE OF THE JAVA SEA: A COMPARISON OF GUNNERY CAPABILITY

When ABDA sortied in force, and encountered the Japanese in the Java Sea on 27 February 1942, the battle was largely decided by torpedoes. However, as we can see, the Japanese also enjoyed a significant superiority over ABDA in terms of gunnery. R. Adm. Takagi's two heavy cruisers, *Haguro* and *Nachi*, enjoyed a significant edge in ordnance over the two ABDA 8in cruisers *Exeter* and *Houston*, partly as the American warship's after turret was out of action. After *Exeter* was badly damaged, and *Houston* hit, the outcome of the battle was never really in doubt. It helped too that the Japanese cruisers had an edge, thanks to the presence of their float planes, the crews of which were able to adjust the fall of shot for the Japanese gunners. Even in the smaller ordnance, of 4.7in to 6in guns, the Japanese enjoyed a significant numerical advantage.

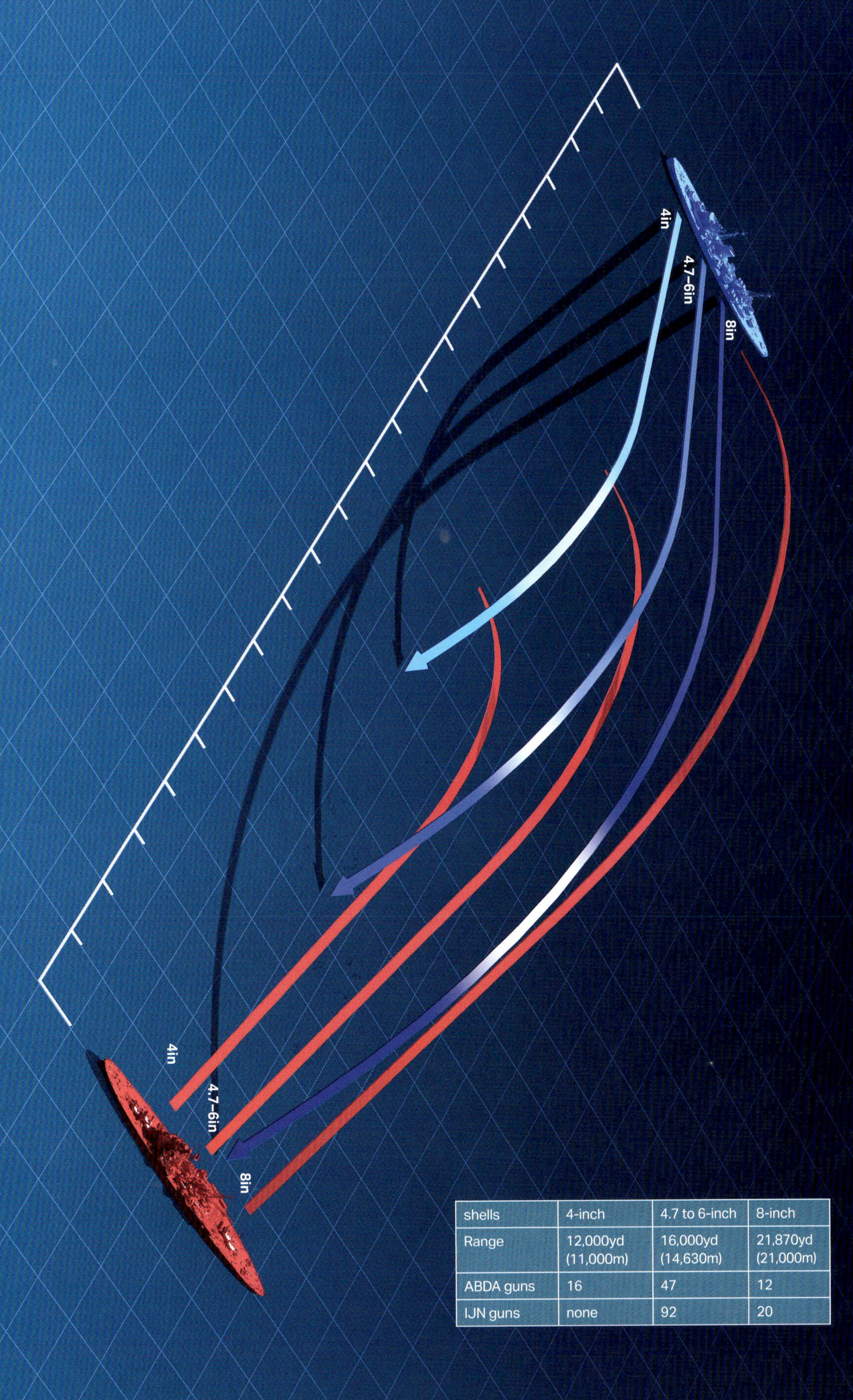

shells	4-inch	4.7 to 6-inch	8-inch
Range	12,000yd (11,000m)	16,000yd (14,630m)	21,870yd (21,000m)
ABDA guns	16	47	12
IJN guns	none	92	20

to mechanical failure, as were the ageing launchers mounted in the Clemson-class vessels.

The much vaunted and top-secret Mark 14 torpedo carried in US Navy submarines had a maximum range of 9,000yds at 30½kts, or 4,500yds at 46kts. In theory this made them more effective than their British-built counterparts. However, they had a flaw. Adm. Hart had high hopes that his submarine force would be able to disrupt any Japanese invasion fleet. His Mark 14 torpedoes had been fitted with the Mark 6 magnetic exploder, which was designed to explode when underneath the keel of a target, even when the torpedo didn't strike it, and so break the target vessel's back.

However, in December 1941, Hart's boats launched 96 'fish' – slang for torpedoes – in 46 attacks off the Philippines. Most of the torpedoes though, didn't work, and only 5 Japanese ships were sunk. Later, it was found that part of the problem was down to poor tactics – at the time the US Navy's method was to attack using hydrophones as a targeting method, rather than the periscope, for fear of giving away the boat's position. As a result, the likelihood of a hit was greatly reduced. Inter-war parsimony had greatly limited the ability of the submariners to practice live firing, so neither problems with tactics nor mechanical systems were exposed until the war began. The result was something of a fiasco.

More serious than poor tactics or inexperienced crew was the mechanical failure of both the Mark 14 torpedo and its magnetic exploder. The torpedo itself was prone to running 11ft deeper than its depth setting, meaning it often passed underneath the target. The detonator was fragile, and prone to malfunction, and it was found it often detonated prematurely. In contrast, the older Mark 10 torpedo used in the older S-class boats proved far

When the Japanese attacked Pearl Harbor, the Clemson-class destroyer USS *Alden* was approaching Singapore, as part of an Anglo-American defence arrangement. The destroyer helped search for survivors from Force Z, before being attached to ABDA. *Alden* was mainly deployed in convoy escort duties, but took part in the Battle of the Java Sea, before withdrawing to Australia, together with three other US destroyers.

more reliable. It was a modified version of the Mark 8 used in the fleet's destroyers. These problems would continue to plague the US Navy until 1943. Effectively, during the campaign for the Philippines and the defence of the Malay barrier, the US Navy appeared to be fighting with one arm tied behind its back.

During the course of the campaign it became apparent that the Japanese torpedoes were in a class of their own. The Type 93 21in torpedo used by Japanese cruisers and destroyers packed an explosive charge of 1,080lb (490kg) – over three times larger than its Allied counterparts. In effect, it virtually guaranteed a hit would result in major damage to its target. Even more impressively, this torpedo, aptly dubbed Long Lance by the Allies, had a maximum speed of 52kts, reducing running time markedly and improving the chances of scoring a hit. Most significant of all though, was its range. The Type 93 torpedo had an effective firing range of 24,000yds at 48kts – around 12nm. Its maximum range was an impressive 44,200yds, at 36kts. This combination of range, speed and destructive power came as a shock to ABDA – the first Allied naval force to experience these torpedoes in action. The Allies simply had nothing that could match Long Lance.

Sensors

Given the large submarine force available to the Japanese Southern Group, ABDA Float faced threats from both above and below the surface. This meant the timely detection of an approaching enemy was crucial. The same, of course, also applied to the air threat, which as Force Z had demonstrated, was probably the most significant danger to the Allied warships. This timely detection meant the use of radar. Unfortunately for ABDA, only two cruisers carried radar. The heavy cruiser *Exeter* was one of them. She carried a Type 279 set, which was fitted early in 1941. Although primarily an air search radar with an effective detection range of 60–80nm, it could also detect surface targets at a range of 15–20nm. This made *Exeter* an extremely useful asset to ABDA Float.

In early 1941, *Perth* was also fitted with an air search radar, a Type 286M set. It had a very limited range of around 16nm, but it also had a surface search capability, at roughly half that range, which essentially gave it the potential ability to detect nearby targets at night. It is likely that *Houston* was also fitted with a CXAM radar, a prototype air search set introduced in mid-1940. This large mattress-shaped device had an air search range of around 30–40nm, and a surface search one of 12nm. *Boise* was fitted with a Mark 3 fire control radar, introduced in 1941, which supported the ship's main 6in battery. However, it also had a limited surface search function, with a detection range of approximately 14nm.

A type 286M was mounted in *Jupiter*, as well as Type 285 fire control radar, which was linked to the destroyer's 4.7in guns. This was also paired with the ship's High-Angle Control System (HACS), which directed AA fire in the British or Commonwealth warships. *Electra* and *Encounter* didn't carry radar: neither did any of the Dutch warships, nor the American destroyers. Still, although only a handful of ABDA warships had radar, it was still an advantage, as at that stage no comparable Japanese device had been developed. In addition, six land-based radar stations sited near Singapore gave warning of enemy air activity within 100nm, but by 15 January when ABDA came into being, these were already out of action. An American land-based SC-270B radar in northern Luzon had a similar range, but it had been put out of action in mid-December.

As for sonar (or ASDIC, as the British called it), all operational destroyers and submarines carried a set, as did the majority of ABDA's cruisers. There was little difference between the British Type 121, 128 or 132 sets carried by the British and the Dutch ships. However, *Tromp* carried a German Persimmon version. These were all slightly superior to the QS sonar in the American Clemson-class destroyers, but all of them were only effective if used aggressively, as part of submarine hunting groups. ABDA though, had no time to perfect such tactics in its multinational force.

AIRCRAFT

For ABDA's naval force to succeed, it needed air cover. In theory, a number of Allied fighters were available, and if the Malay Barrier were to be held, then these would need to play their part. In practice though, ABDA Float could expect very little practical support from ABDA Air. While much of the problem lay with ABDA's impossibly convoluted chains of commands, a lack of suitable aircraft played its part too. This was almost entirely due to the staggering losses suffered by the Allied air forces during the opening weeks of the war.

Before 7 December, Gen. Brereton's Far East Air Force (FEAF) maintained a sizeable force of fighters and bombers in the Philippines. Around 100 modern Curtiss P-40s were deployed there, as was a bombardment group of 24 B-17 bombers. Gen. MacArthur considered the islands safe from air attack, but he was swiftly proved wrong. On 12 December, when Clark Field was bombed, FEAF lost over 100 aircraft, including most of its bombers. After that, subsequent Japanese air operations led to the destruction of almost all of Brereton's command. However, by 15 January, some 20 B-17 and B-24 bombers (or rather their LB-30 export version) were reformed in Java, together with 26 P-40s. These would form the core of the USAAF's contribution to ABDA Air. The P-40 was the most modern Allied fighter available in the region, and in theory it should have performed well, were it not for the problem the USAAF had in maintaining these aircraft.

The main anti-aircraft platform of the Dutch cruiser HNLMS *De Ruyter* atop the ship's after superstructure. It carried four Swedish-designed 40mm (1.57in) Bofors automatic air defence guns in single mountings. This was arguably the best AA weapon in ABDA Striking Force, and improved versions soon became commonplace aboard Allied warships.

RAF Far East Command, which included British, Australian and New Zealand squadrons, was charged with the defence of Malaya and Singapore. At its disposal were around 60 operational American-built Brewster Buffalo fighters. This was a slow, manoeuvrable aircraft, and ill-matched against more modern Japanese counterparts. As for bombers, the RAF had 47 Bristol Blenheim light bombers, 29 Vickers Vildebeest torpedo bombers and around 20 Lockheed Hudson light bombers. From 8 December, these would be pitched against the Imperial Japanese Air Force, and losses mounted steadily both on the ground and in the air.

In theory, the Vildebeests would have been useful as maritime strike aircraft, but these obsolete biplanes had already been sacrificed in an attack on 26 December. By the time Singapore fell in mid-February, what remained of RAF Far East Command had been evacuated to India. However, in mid-January, almost 100 Hawker Hurricane fighters arrived, and eventually they were relocated to Java and Sumatra. These fast, modern fighters would form the core of the RAF's contribution to ABDA Air.

As for the Dutch, the Royal Netherlands Indies Army Air Division possessed just under a hundred each of operational fighters and bombers, and 34 reconnaissance planes. This sizeable force was divided into five air groups – three of bombers and two of fighters. Most of these were based in Java and Sumatra, with some squadrons deployed elsewhere, such as Ambon and Tarakan. The fighters were all American-built, a mix of Curtiss P-36 Hawks, Curtiss Wright 21s and Brewster Buffalos – the most numerous of the three types. Most of the bombers were also American Martin B-10s, a twin-engined aircraft that had a respectable payload, but suffered from a lack of speed. Still, during the campaign these would be used in maritime strikes, albeit without much success.

The Dutch Navy also operated aircraft. The Marine Luchtvaart Dienst (MLD) maintained a number of flying boats, which were used for maritime reconnaissance, air-sea rescue and anti-submarine patrols. Until the war, these were German-built seaplanes – around 20 Fokker and 30 Dornier aircraft, the most common being the three-engined Dornier Do-24 float plane. However, from 1941, a number of American Catalina flying boats entered service with the MLD, and just over 20 were in service when the war began. In addition, the cruisers *De Ruyter* and *Tromp* were provided with catapults, designed to operate the smaller Fokker C-XI W float plane, eight of which were in service in the East Indies at the start of the war.

The naval defence of the Malay Barrier was only practicable with air support. The Japanese air bases in French Indochina and later the Philippines placed their greatly superior air assets within reach of the barrier and its naval defenders. Throughout January, the steady advance of the Japanese into the Dutch East Indies meant that by the end of the month, the Japanese were able to establish forward air bases in Borneo, the Celebes and eventually in Malaya. Consequently, the Japanese were able to dominate the skies over the Java Sea and the islands of the Malay Barrier. Outnumbered and often out-performed, ABDA Air was hard pressed to protect its own aircraft and airfields, let alone ABDA's naval strike force. So, for all practical purposes, the warships would have to defend themselves.

The heavy cruiser HMS *Exeter*, pictured in action off Banka Island on the morning of 15 February, while under air attack. Unusually, these were bomb-armed 'Kate' torpedo bombers, operating from the light carrier IJNS *Ryujo*. *Exeter* was fitted with a Type 279 air search radar, and at least on this occasion a combination of high-speed manoeuvring and fire from the ship's AA guns were enough to thwart these attacks.

HOW THE FLEET OPERATED

DOCTRINE AND COMMAND

In essence, ABDA COM Striking Force was a straightforward entity. It was a multinational naval squadron, made up of warships from its four component nations: the United States, Great Britain, the Netherlands (or rather its overseas dominions in the Dutch East Indies) and Australia. Its commander was a 52-year-old Dutchman, R. Adm. Karel Doorman (1889–1942), of the Royal Netherlands Navy. Born in Utrecht, he attended the naval college in Den Helder, then joined the navy when he was 21. After a spell in the East Indies, he returned home, and specialized as a naval aviator. He was made a knight in 1922, but when injury ended his flying career he returned to the East Indies, where he held a staff post in Batavia (now Jakarta). He married, divorced and remarried there, but in 1926 he returned to sea for a couple of years before returning to the Netherlands for another staff appointment.

He was given his first command, the minelayer HNLMS *Prins van Oranje*, in 1932, and was subsequently given command of destroyers, first *Witte de With* and then *Evertsen*. More shore jobs followed, but in 1938, after his promotion to *Kapitein-ter-zee* (Captain), he returned to the East Indies to take command of the cruiser *Sumatra*. A year later, he was given command of *Java*, before being named the new head of naval aviation in the East Indies. On 16 May, six days after Germany had invaded the Netherlands, Doorman was made a *Schout-bij-nacht* (R. Adm.), and the following month he raised his flag aboard the cruiser *De Ruyter* in Sourabaya. This in turn led to him being appointed the commander of ABDA's naval striking force in February 1942.

Before becoming Commander of ABDA Float in mid-January 1942, Admiral Thomas C. Hart USN was the Commander-in-Chief of the US Asiatic Fleet. He was an intelligent and highly able commander, but when he proved unable to counter the numbers and quality of his Japanese opponents, he was relieved of his command.

Doorman was a difficult man to get on with, as he was very demanding, both of himself and others, and was quick to show his disagreement with superiors, and his want of patience for subordinates. While he lacked combat experience, or even an extensive record of sea service, Doorman was intelligent and able. He was also willing to fight regardless of the odds against him, and while privately pessimistic, he hid this from his officers and men.

Doorman might have held ABDA's seagoing command, but he was the final step in a sizeable and complex chain of command. ABDA itself was the result of a hastily cobbled together structure, created after the first Japanese attack, but based on talks which had taken place before the outbreak of hostilities. It was strange that the German invasion of the Netherlands in May 1940 didn't lead directly to the development of plans for mutual defence in South-East Asia with the British and the French. By November, when talks began between British, Australian, American and Dutch representatives, the Netherlands had capitulated, and the Dutch East Indies had been left to their own devices. The following February, a conference was held in Singapore, but it, like the previous meeting, fell short of any formal defence agreement.

It was only in April 1941 that a mutual defence policy was discussed in any detail, but the operational specifics weren't agreed on. However, this led to the development of a structure that August, although even then the USA refused to be drawn into any cast-iron commitment. A new conference was due to be held in Manila in December, but the Japanese struck first. The result was a reactionary, ad-hoc arrangement between the various Allies, created while the Japanese were conquering Manila, Hong Kong and Malaya, and sinking Force Z. In early January, the Arcadia Conference was held in Washington DC, where the American, British, Dutch and Australian joint command was formally proposed, with the British Gen. Sir Archibald Wavell named as its Commander-in-Chief. However, it wasn't until Wavell arrived in Batavia on 10 January that the arrangement was ratified, and ABDA Command formally came into being five days later, on the 15th.

By then it was really too late to create any policy for mutual defence. The Philippines had been largely overrun, and the British and Commonwealth garrison of Malaya had fallen back to Singapore. Ironically, the only agreed strategy was based on a now completely outdated British one, which called for the defence of the Malay Barrier. While the name referred to the curving line of islands which stretched from Singapore to Timor, which included Sumatra, Java and Bali, the plan had already been undermined by the Japanese conquest of Malaya. The enemy were now pressing on Singapore, and

Admiral Hart was succeeded as Commander of ABDA Float by Vice-Admiraal (V. Adm.) Conrad Helfrich RNN, who was already commander of the Dutch East Indies Squadron. However, Helfrich continued to rely on R. Adm. Doorman to lead his Striking Force.

15° N
95° E
100° E
105° E
110° E
115° E
120° E
125° E
130° E
10° N
5° N
Equator
5° S
10° S
15° S
BURMA
Bangkok
INDOCHINA
OCCUPIED DECEMBER 1941
Camranh Bay
Andaman Is.
Port Blair
Gulf of Siam
Saigon
South China Sea
Manila
24 Dec
11 Dec
PHILIPPINES
SIAM
Palawan
Mindanao
Davao
20 Dec
PACIFIC OCEAN
Nicobar Is.
8 Dec
19 Jan
Labuan
16 Dec
Sabang
Panang
Kota Bharu
Sandakan
British North Borneo
Brunei
MALAYA
Malacca Strait
Kuantan
Natuna
11 Jan
Tarakan
Medan
15 Feb
24 Dec
24 Jan
Sarawak
Moratai
Menado
Kuching
Singapore
Molucca Passage
SUMATRA
14 Feb
24 Jan
Dutch Borneo
Ceram Sea
Padang
Balikpapan
Strait of Makassar
Dutch New Guinea
Banka
Celebes
12 Jan
24 Jan
Maluku
Palemban
Kendari
Amboina
1 March
Java Sea
9 Feb
Makassar
Bawean
1 March
Banda Sea
INDIAN OCEAN
Batavia
Sunda Strait
Flores Sea
Bandoeng
JAVA
Soerabaya
19 Feb
Tjilatjap
Bali
Dili
20 Feb
Timor
Bali Strait
Lombok Strait
Kupang
Timor Sea
N
Darwin
AUSTRALIA
0
500 nautical miles
500km
ABDA naval base
Secondary naval base
British and Commonwealth possession before 7 December 1941
Dutch possession before 7 December 1941
United States possession before 7 December 1941
Japanese secondary naval base
Japanese assaults, December 1941–March 1942

while the British felt their island fortress could be held, it was poorly defended on the landward side, and so its fall was arguably a matter of time. If Singapore went, the whole barrier crumbled, as the Japanese would have breached its western end. Still, for the moment, it was a strategy to which ABDA agreed to stick.

The command structure of ABDA was over-complicated, as each participating nation had to be represented in some way, and most still retained their own national command structures, which would run in tandem with the ABDA ones. While Wavell was the Commander-in-Chief, with his temporary headquarters in Batavia, the overall naval commander of what was known as ABDA Float was Adm. Thomas C. Hart of the US Navy. Hart's Deputy was R. Adm. Arthur Palliser of the Royal Navy. Their headquarters was in the Imperial Hotel in Lembang, 60 miles east of Batavia. However, the Royal Netherlands Navy already had a naval commander in the Dutch East Indies, *Luitenant-Admiraal* (V. Adm.) Conrad Helfrich, whose authority remained separate from ABDA, who was also based in Batavia. The British also had their own area commander, V. Adm. Sir Geoffrey Layton, Commander-in-Chief of the Eastern Fleet, which was based at Colombo in Ceylon.

The Americans also had a conflict of command, as when Adm. Hart's US Asiatic Fleet was officially disbanded, and its remains incorporated into ABDA Float, a separate naval command was established by the US Navy, answerable directly to the Commander-in-Chief of US Naval Forces in the Pacific. This command was known as US Naval Forces South Pacific, which was commanded by V. Adm. William A. Glassford USN. So, the British, Dutch and Americans all retained an overlapping naval organization throughout the campaign.

The same problem existed with the air element, ABDA Air. It was under the command of ACM Sir Richard Pierse of the RAF, who adopted procedures for all the national elements of his command. This had the unfortunate effect of severing the close direct relationships between the Dutch Air Force and Dutch Navy in the East Indies. However, all three countries also retained their own national air commands: under Pierse, Lt Gen. Lewis H. Brereton of the USAAF and Lt Gen. van Oyten of the Dutch Air Force. A similar structure plagued ABDA Arm, the ground forces element of ABDA, which was under the command of Lt Gen. Hein ter Poorten of the Netherlands East Indies Army. In time, this ludicrous command situation could have been simplified and made to work. Unfortunately time wasn't an asset ABDA possessed.

On 12 February, V. Adm. Hart was unexpectedly notified by the Navy Department that he would be relieved of his post as commander of ABDA Float. Verification of this arrived on 16 February, at which point the command was transferred to V. Adm. Helfrich. The reason given for this was the American admiral's health. However, his subordinates, having witnessed the agility of their 63-year-old commander, were in no doubt this was nonsense. It transpired that this was a political decision, following pressure from the Dutch commanders in the theatre, including from Hart's successor. Hart was a well-respected commander, a submariner who had risen through the ranks by merit. When President Roosevelt awarded him a Gold Star to add to his Distinguished Service Medal, he said Hart was 'characterised by unfailing judgement and sound decision, coupled with marked moral courage, in the face of discouraging surroundings and complex associations'.

Finally, on 22 February, following the dissolution of ABDA, Helfrich was flown to Ceylon, where he was tasked with preparing for the Dutch recapture of the East Indies. At that point, Commodore John Collins of the Royal Australian Navy assumed command of all British and Commonwealth forces in the area. With no other suitable label at the time, this command was dubbed China Force. In 1941, as the commander of the cruiser HMAS *Sydney*, Collins had distinguished himself in the Mediterranean by sinking an Italian cruiser. A natural leader and a skilled organiser, it was Collins rather than Helfrich who organized the evacuation of Java in the aftermath of the Japanese invasion. He left Java on one of the last ships out, on 8 March. Afterwards, Collins became Senior Naval Officer, Western Australia, charged with defending the country from an invasion, which fortunately never came.

V. Adm. William A. Glassford USN led Task Force 5 Striking Force, attached to ABDA, while Adm. Hart commanded all of ABDA Float. It was Glassford who orchestrated the Balikpapan attack, and from 4 February he assumed official command of all of the US Navy's element of ABDA Float.

The one real success of ABDA Float was the ability of the component navies to work together, and to adopt a common doctrine. For the most part this was worked out between Adm. Hart and his deputy R. Adm. Palliser, and the two Dutch commanders of import, V. Adm. Helfrich and R. Adm. Doorman. Essentially, as Dutch naval methods of manoeuvring and methods of engagement

ABDA STRIKING FORCE ORGANIZATION CHART

ABDA Combined Striking Force was the operational element of ABDA Float, the naval arm of ABDA COM. Like ABDA itself, ABDA Float was made up of elements from all four participating nations – the United States of America, Great Britain, the Commonwealth of Australia and the Netherlands. More accurately though, as the Netherlands had been under German occupation since May 1940, the country was represented by the colonial government of the Dutch East Indies and their fleet by warships of the Dutch East Indies Squadron.

The composition of ABDA Striking Force varied throughout the campaign, as vessels were detached to form convoy escorts or for other duties. As a result, the only true core of the Striking Force was the Dutch light cruiser *De Ruyter*, flagship of its commander, R. Adm. Doorman. He though, could draw on whatever ABDA Float vessels were available, subject to the approval of ABDA Float's commander-in-chief.

In addition, the Royal Navy and the Royal Australian Navy were united under one command, and it, as well as the other two participating navies, maintained their own national commander, who had the authority to temporarily deploy their nation's vessels as required. Somehow though, this complicated multi-national organisation worked, up to a point. If it had existed for longer, it might have been welded onto an efficient multi-national standing naval force. Unfortunately, the Japanese never allowed it the respite it needed to become fully established.

Cruisers
Houston
Boise
Marblehead
Destroyers
US Navy
Adm Hart USN
(Vice-Adm Glassford USN from 4 February)
Houston: Northampton class heavy cruiser, *Boise*: Brooklyn class light cruiser, *Marblehead*: Omaha class light cruiser
All destroyers: Clemson class destroyers, c.1920
Royal Netherlands Navy
Vice-Adm Helfrich RNN
De Ruyter: De Ruyer-class light cruiser, *Java* and *Tromp*: Java class light cruisers
All destroyers: Admiraal class destroyers
(*Evertsen, Kortenaer, Piet Hein, Van Ghent:* Van Ghent sub-class,
Banckert, Van Nes, Wiitte de With: Van Gelen sub-class)

ABDA Float – SURFACE FORCES
Adm Hart USN in Command
(Vice-Adm Helfrich RNN from 16 February)

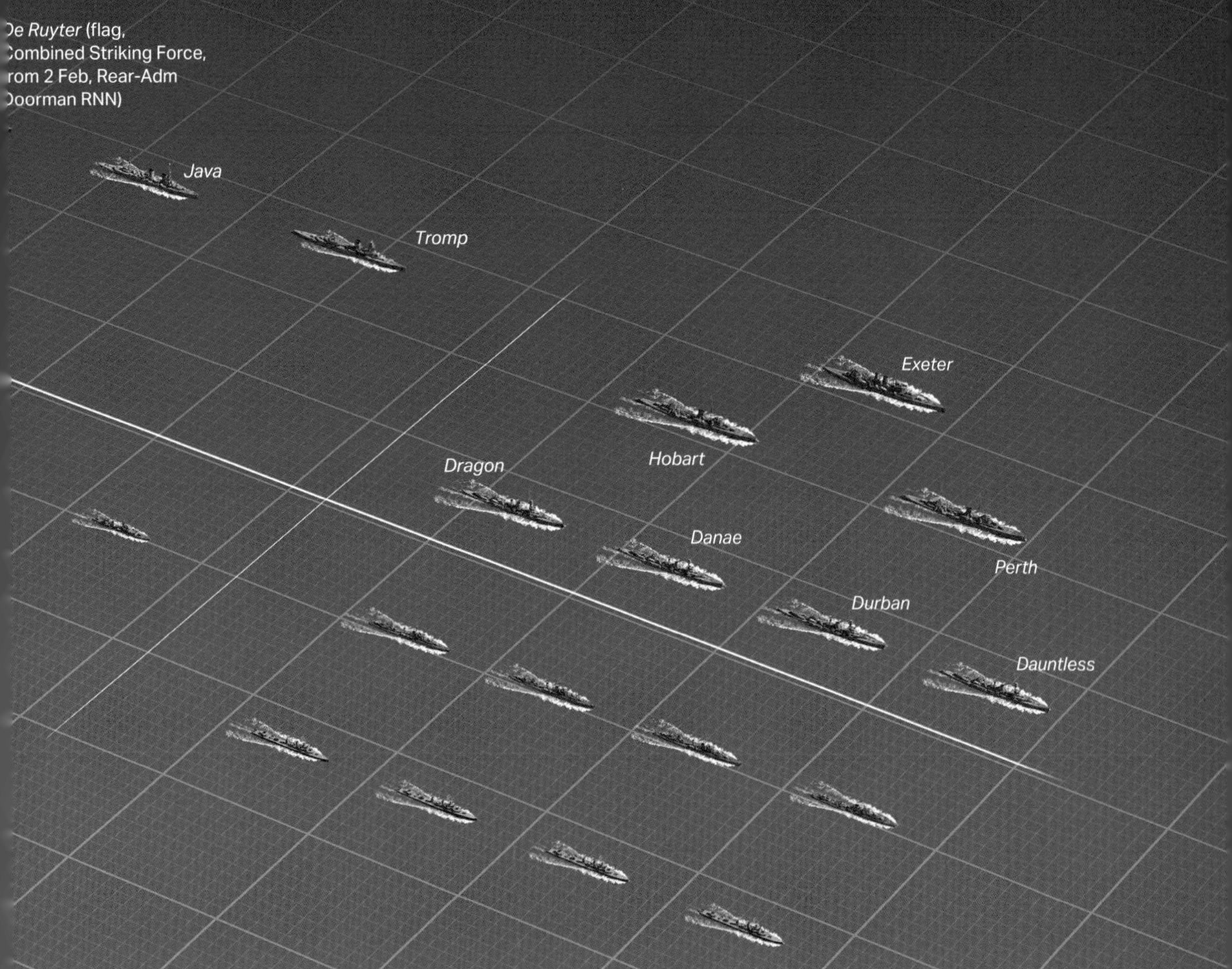

De Ruyter (flag, Combined Striking Force, from 2 Feb, Rear-Adm Doorman RNN)

Java

Tromp

Exeter

Hobart

Dragon

Danae

Perth

Durban

Dauntless

Royal Navy (and Royal Australian Navy)
Adm Sir Geoffrey Layton RN
(Comm. Collins RAN from 22 February)

Exeter: York class heavy cruiser, *Hobart, Perth*: Sydney class (or improved Leander class) light cruiser

Dragon, Danae, Durban, Dauntless: D-class light cruisers

Electra, Encounter, Express: E-class destroyers; *Jupiter*: J,K, M class destroyers

Scout, Stronghold, Tenados, Thanet: Admiralty S-class c.1920

were based largely on the Royal Navy model, this was adopted, and the US Navy's warships which formed part of ABDA Striking Force adopted these methods. In practice there was little difference between the four national elements, especially as the Royal Australian Navy already used British doctrine and procedures. For those few units that formed part of ABDA Float but weren't included in the Striking Force, they were allowed to use their existing procedures. However, as most of these were either Australian, British or Dutch, this wasn't a problem.

Each navy had its own rules of engagement, but again, these were broadly similar, and any differences were quickly dealt with by Hart, Palliser and Doorman. However, one area where there was a tactical discrepancy was in response to a determined enemy air attack. While the British and Australians had learned their lesson in the Mediterranean, they preferred to concentrate their ships, and therefore their AA firepower. At this stage, the Americans and Dutch did the opposite, and preferred to disperse their ships, on the grounds that this would also split up the attacking aircraft into penny packets, which would be less successful than if attacking en masse. In the end, when ABDA Striking Force first carried out an operation of its own, with its doomed sortie into the Flores Sea between Java and Celebes, the weakness of this American and Dutch doctrine was revealed. After that, the British and Australian method was adopted by the other two navies in the Striking Force.

INTELLIGENCE, COMMUNICATION AND DECEPTION

By 15 January, when ABDA came into being, the Allies knew what was in store for them. In the Philippines, the Americans had lost the archipelago, save for Bataan, which was under siege, and the adjacent fortress island of Corregidor. There was no hope of reinforcements, and the eventual surrender of the remaining American forces there seemed inevitable. Meanwhile, most of Malaya had fallen to the Japanese. The British and Commonwealth troops defending the Malay peninsula had been driven back towards the island of Singapore, off its southern tip, and the Japanese were now 100 miles from the city. Radio intercepts reported that the Japanese had withdrawn troops, ships and aircraft from the two theatres, and were deploying them in an assault on the Dutch East Indies.

This of course, was already underway. Landings in Sarawak, Brunei, North Borneo and then Tarakan off Dutch Borneo had already taken place, so too had Japanese landings at Menado in the north of Celebes. What this meant from the perspective of gathering intelligence was that little could be expected from either theatre, as they were too embroiled fighting their own battles for survival. This was particularly true when it came to air reconnaissance. The best ABDA could expect was reports generated from either Corregidor or Singapore, reporting any relevant Japanese troop or ship movements, though this wasn't the only source

The brand new Salmon-class submarine USS *Stingray* was attached to the US Asiatic Fleet in late 1941. After operating in defence of the Philippines, the boat was attached to ABDA and sailed on two war patrols in the waters of the Dutch East Indies, before being withdrawn to Hawaii. Although the boat carried out several attacks, malfunctioning torpedoes meant that *Stingray* didn't sink any enemy vessels until later in 1942.

of intelligence. Any Japanese activity in the East Indies was likely to be reported to Batavia by local Dutch officials in Dutch Borneo, the Celebes archipelago, Ceram and the Molucca Islands, and Dutch New Guinea. Inevitably though, once the Japanese invaded these places, this source of information would cease.

That left the Allies with the options of using intelligence based on radio intercepts or else sighting reports by patrolling Allied submarines and through air reconnaissance. In some ways ABDA was fortunate, in that before the war, the Dutch air force and navy had cooperated closely, and maritime air reconnaissance was considered an important part of the defence of the Dutch East Indies. However, the creation of ABDA Air meant that Dutch air units were placed under a centralized command, led by a British commander who knew little about these arrangements. Instead, he saw the Dutch squadrons as a vital component of his air defence plans for the theatre.

In early February, ABDA Air headquarters was moved from Lembang in Java, where it shared a building with ABDA Float, to Bandung, a few miles away. This didn't seem important at the time, but it effectively led to delays and lost communications between the two elements of ABDA. To make matters worse, while the Royal Netherlands Navy maintained its own naval air service, its headquarters was also moved from ABDA Float's building, and moved into its own administrative centre in Bandung. This would inevitably lead to delays in passing on vital time-sensitive sighting reports.

THE OPERATIONAL CONSTRICTION OF ABDA, 15 JANUARY–16 FEBRUARY 1942

When ABDA was formed in mid-January 1942 the only Japanese air bases in the area were on Mindanao in the Philippines and in Sarawak on Borneo. Gradually though, the Japanese tentacles reached ever further into the East Indies. The establishment of a major air base at Kendari in the south of Celebes ensured Japanese control of the skies over the Flores Sea, while to the east the advance through the Malay peninsula, followed by the fall of Singapore and Japanese landings in Sumatra, meant that they also controlled the Java Sea. Meanwhile, the two Japanese invasion groups continued their pressure on Java from both east and west. A Japanese carrier attached to V. Adm. Ozawa's Western Invasion Group, and the main Japanese carrier force's operations around Timor, ensured ABDA lost control of the skies, and with it control of the waters surrounding Java. By late February, any ABDA sortie from Java risked annihilation, either from the sea or the air.

MALAYA
Western Invasion Group –
V. Adm. Ozawa
Jesselton
Mindanao
Davao
by 10 Feb
South China Sea
BRUNEI
Brunei
NORTH BORNEO
Singapore
fall 15 Feb
(island)
SARAWAK
Eastern Invasion Group –
V. Adm. Takashi
Celebes Sea
Kuching,
by 15 Jan
Tarakan (island)
Sumatra
DUTCH BORNEO
Menado
Pelambang,
by 16 Feb
Balikpapan,
by 29 Jan
Makassar
Strait
Celebes
Java Sea
Banjarmasin
Batavia
Banda Sea
Tjilitjap
Kendari,
by 28 Jan
Makassar
Java
Sourabaya
AIR LIMIT
MALAYA
Flores Sea
Bali
Sumbawa
Flores
AIR LIMIT KENDARI

Despite this, ABDA Striking Force could rely on maritime patrols carried out by ABDA and the Dutch Naval Air Service, thanks to the collection of a number of suitable air formations. These were of little use to the air defence of Java, and so were allowed to continue operating air patrols in search of Japanese naval forces. An air reconnaissance group was based around the float planes of the Royal Netherlands East Indies Naval Air Service, which was partly deployed in small flight-sized groups in a number of East Indies airfields, although the bulk were concentrated at Morokrembangan naval airfield near Sourabaya, or at Tanjong Priok naval base by Batavia. Other flights were based from Emmershaven in south-eastern Sumatra to Ambon in the Banda Islands, including Tarakan and Pontianak in Dutch Borneo. While these flights were still operational, they were able to pass on sighting reports of Japanese naval movements to ABDA Air's headquarters.

The Dutch were also supported by Patrol Wing 10, a squadron of Catalina flying boats of the US Navy, and by 205 Squadron of the RAF, which also operated Catalinas. These were based on Java. In addition, the Dutch Air Force continued to operate fighter sweeps across the southern portion of the South China Sea, as well as the Java Sea and Flores Sea until the airbases in Sumatra and then Java were overrun. However, by late February almost all of these air assets had been destroyed, and what remained of ABDA Striking Force's warships had to make their own assumptions of Japanese naval deployments, while planning their own escape from Java.

Another source of intelligence was ABDA's force of American and Dutch submarines. These formed patrol lines off ports used by the Japanese, or patrolled the waters of chokepoints or invasion routes in the Makassar Strait, the waters around the Celebes archipelago, or the waters of the South China Sea between Singapore and Banka Island. Throughout the campaign, this remained the most reliable form of intelligence gathering.

Accurate intelligence gathering though, relied on good communications. While the naval bases at Singapore, Tanjong Priok and Sourabaya all had good radio facilities, these were all subject to attack during the campaign, which degraded their efficiency. As a result, ABDA Striking Force was forced to rely on secondary shore facilities in Sumatra, Borneo and Java, or long-range

The submarine HNLMS *K-13*, one of 16 boats maintained by the Dutch in the East Indies. However, after a battery explosion in Singapore on 21 December, *K-13* was towed to Sourabaya, for repairs. These were incomplete by 2 March, and so the boat was scuttled before it fell into enemy hands.

communication links to Freemantle in Australia and Trincomalee in Ceylon, where signals could be passed on either to or from ABDA's warships and bases. The warships themselves were all well served, and thanks to the Dutch ability to master English, there was little problem in verbal communications.

Signalling systems varied between navies, but generally the Dutch methods were adopted by all the other nationalities. This presented little problem, as it was based on the British system of communication using signal flags and by signalling lamps. These had the advantage of avoiding the interception of radio communications, either between ships or between flagships and their base, and the attendant risk of giving away the squadron's position to the enemy. In other waters, the same could be true in reverse, with Allied listening stations being used to triangulate enemy radio signals, to locate an enemy force at sea. Unfortunately, this wasn't available to ABDA. While the British had a small chain of listening stations on Singapore and Malaya, these were rendered useless following the Japanese advance down the Malay peninsula. The Dutch had never built such a network, and so the naval commanders of the Striking Force and ABDA Float had to rely on other sources for their intelligence of Japanese ship movements.

While the art of deception had been used by the British and Australians in the Mediterranean, using false radio reports of friendly shipping movements, or other forms of subterfuge, it appears nothing of this kind was attempted by ABDA. Frankly, it had enough to face merely surviving the succession of hammer blows delivered to it by the Japanese. The closest it came to the Allies practising the art of deception was the camouflage of ships, either while under repair at ports in Java or when attempting to escape from the Japanese following the collapse of organized naval resistance. Besides, for the most part, the Japanese had a fairly good idea where ABDA Striking Force was at any one time, and with air superiority it was able to maintain regular reconnaissance flights over Java and its adjacent waters; so Japanese commanders remained well informed about the capabilities of Allied warships and could plan their own deployments accordingly.

LOGISTICS AND FACILITIES

Before war came to the Dutch East Indies, the Royal Netherlands Navy maintained two main naval bases in the region, Tanjong Priok and Sourabaya, both of which were on the north coast of Java, on the island's western and eastern ends respectively, facing the Java Sea. There was also a secondary base at Tjilatjap on the southern coast of Java, which looked out on the Indian Ocean. In addition, the Dutch maintained small naval facilities at Tarakan, the island off the eastern coast of Dutch Borneo, at Emmershaven on the east coast of Sumatra and at Amboina on Ambon Island, one of the Banda Islands, which faced the Banda Sea.

In theory, the Royal Navy maintained a major naval base at Singapore, while the US Asiatic Fleet was based at Cavite in the Philippines, on the southern outskirts of Manila, and looking out onto Manila Bay. However, by the time ABDA had been formed, both of these bases were no longer available – Singapore was under regular air attack and threatened by the advance of the Japanese army, and Cavite had also been extensively bombed and then overrun by the Japanese. So, the only Allied port of any significance in the theatre was Freemantle in Western Australia, the port serving the city of Perth. The Royal Australian Navy maintained a small base there. During the campaign, Darwin in Australia's Northern Territory was also used as a makeshift naval base, albeit one with little in the way of facilities.

The real drawback of the three Dutch ports in Java was their almost chronic lack of spare parts, fuel and ordnance. Since the fall of the Netherlands in May 1940, the Dutch authorities and military commanders in the East Indies had worked hard to make their colony more self-sufficient. In naval terms, this meant the improvement of ports and the manufacturing of parts and ordnance locally, in Java. However, this was a slow process, and relied on raw materials which were in short supply in 1941 and early 1942. Still, when ABDA was formed it had no choice but to assume control of these three key naval harbours, and to continue the work of making them more resilient and adaptable. Even then, they were hard pressed to deal with the steady stream of damaged warships needing repairs as the war went on.

Sourabaya

In 1942, Sourabaya was the main base for the Dutch Navy in the East Indies. Since the 18th century, Sourabaya had been the largest city in the East Indies, with a pre-war population of around 330,000. In 1921, work began on modernizing the small Dutch naval base there, which lay at the northern side of the city, on the shore of the Madung Strait. At its heart was a drydock capable of housing 5,000-ton vessels. There was also a smaller 3,000-ton drydock, while a second slightly smaller one had just been finished by the time the Japanese invaded. Dredging completed shortly before the war allowed heavy cruisers to access to the dockyard and the largest dry dock, which greatly boosted the value of the base to ABDA.

Unusually, the drydocks weren't operated by the Dutch Navy, but by a private company, the Sourabaya Drydock Corporation, as private funds had been used in its construction. Extensive quayside facilities and adjacent moorings provided space for much of the Dutch naval squadron in the pre-war East Indies and then served a similar role for ABDA. In addition, administrative buildings, a fuelling station, repair workshops, water storage tanks, warehouses

The light cruiser USS *Marblehead* entering Tjilatjap harbour on 6 February, after sustaining damage in the Flores Sea two days earlier. The heavy cruiser USS *Houston*, which was in the same action, is already alongside. *Houston* suffered damage to her after 8in turret, which rendered the cruiser out of action for the remainder of the campaign.

The Clemson-class destroyer USS *Peary* and the Northampton-class cruiser USS *Houston*, pictured in Darwin Roads, in mid-February, after engaging in convoy work. On 19 February, *Peary* was sunk there during a massed air attack by 242 Japanese aircraft. *Houston* was lost off the Sunda Strait early on 1 March.

and recreation facilities were provided in the dockyard. Across the Madura Strait, on Madura Island, a factory produced sea mines and manufactured shells. However, the materials for these became scarce following the fall of the Netherlands in May 1940.

In peacetime, these quay facilities at Sourabaya were also used by civilian vessels. In addition, in the summer of 1940, facilities were built there for smaller craft, such as motor torpedo boats. Unfortunately, the naval base lacked adequate protection, although an artificial island for a gun battery was under construction when the Japanese invaded. However, AA protection was provided around both the dockyard and other adjacent facilities.

In 1925 a *Marine Vliegkamp* ('flying boat base') was built at Morokrembangan, a little to the west of the dockyard, with direct access to the sheltered Lamong Gulf, a bay on the south side of the Madura Strait. While its emphasis was on the maintenance of naval flying boats, the base also contained runways and hangars for conventional aircraft, and for use by trainee pilots. It also shared its facilities with a civilian airline, Royal Dutch East Indies Airways, which maintained scheduled flights from the airfield to destinations as far afield as Tarakan and Darwin. The site now forms part of the Indonesian Navy's Juanta naval base.

During the 1920s, the Dutch also built a submarine base at Sourabaya, on the opposite side of the dockyard from Morokrembangan. This was the first purpose-built base of its kind in the Dutch East Indies and allowed the Royal Netherlands Navy to expand its submarine fleet in the region. This included repair facilities, torpedo maintenance workshops, ordnance stores, administration buildings and barracks, and leisure facilities for submarine crews. When US submarines were based there following the US Asiatic Fleet's withdrawal from Cavite, the submariners were favourably impressed by what the Dutch Navy had built up there. Finally, there was a marine barracks, close to the centre of the city, called Gebeng (now Guneng), which was the major base for the Dutch marines in the East Indies.

Tanjong Priok

The second-largest port in Java during this period, Tanjong Priok, served as the port for Batavia, the capital of the Dutch East Indies, which lay five miles to the north-east of the colonial capital. It was primarily a commercial port, although Dutch naval facilities had existed there since the mid-18th century. The port was rebuilt during the late 19th century, and approach channels dredged in order to permit access to large commercial vessels. The Royal Dutch Navy expanded its facilities there, which included naval access to an 8,000-ton and a 4,000-ton capacity floating dry dock, run by a private company. However, by 1942, most naval activity took place at Sourabaya, 400 miles to the east.

Still, limited naval facilities were maintained at Tanjong Priok, such as a naval quay and jetty, refuelling facilities, and some storage and warehouse buildings, as well as administrative buildings. These were protected by a number of AA emplacements and by a coastal battery. In 1919, the Dutch Air Force established an airfield there, which was then transferred to the Royal Netherlands Navy, which used it as a flying base for floatplanes. However, by May 1940, it was in poor condition, having been out of service for several years. It was restored in 1941 though, and fuel and storage facilities were added, to create a useful float plane base for up to 20 flying boats.

After December 1941, the port became crowded with ships fleeing the Japanese expansion through South-East Asia, and trade through the port increased. However, the naval needs of Tanjong Priok weren't ignored, as the port was refurbished and expanded during the months leading up to the Japanese invasion of Java. The short-lived Western Striking Force was formed there, using obsolete British and Dutch warships, and it also served as a refuge for ABDA warships seeking a temporary haven.

Tjilatjap

Finally, on the south coast of Java, a small Dutch naval base, which provided decent anchorage and was sheltered by the prison island of Nusakambangan, was established at Tjilatjap (now Cilacap). Unfortunately, the narrow and winding approach channel to the harbour remained a problem, and limited the use of Tjilatjap by both commercial and large naval vessels. However, when the Japanese attacks began it became of crucial importance, being the only Dutch port of size on the south side of the island. Again, the dredged channel only allowed access to ships with a draft of less than 10 metres, and once in the port there were only four small piers, which precluded its use by larger cruisers.

Still, the port had limited repair and refuelling facilities there and so served as a haven for damaged ABDA ships, at a time when the island's two larger ports were subjected to heavy aerial attacks. While Tjilatjap was protected by a coastal fort of 19th-century vintage, equipped with a small battery of antiquated guns, air defences remained minimal. As happened in Java's other ports, in the aftermath of the Japanese offensive there was increased use of the port by cargo vessels, ABDA naval units fleeing other ports and ships sent to Tjilatjap for repair. By then though, many Indonesian workers had left their jobs in the harbour, as it had been subjected to a series of Japanese air attacks. However, following the Japanese invasion of Java, the port proved of great use as ships used it to evacuate civilian and military refugees to the safety of Australia.

COMBAT AND ANALYSIS

ABDA COMMAND IN COMBAT

Balikpapan

The Japanese didn't even have the courtesy to wait for the Allies to get their new ABDA force established. On 10 January, Dutch patrol aircraft sighted a Japanese transport force at sea to the south of the Philippines. In fact there were two of them at sea that morning, one heading for Dutch Borneo, and the other for Celebes. At 0100hrs the next morning, 11 January, one of these invasion forces appeared off Tarakan, a small oil-producing island off the north-east coast of Dutch Borneo. It consisted of 13 transport ships, 11 destroyers and several other smaller warships, all under the command of R. Adm. Hirose, of V. Adm. Kondo's Southern Force.

As the Japanese amphibious force landed from 0220hrs, under the cover of a naval bombardment, the oil installations there were set ablaze, and the island's

THE BALIKPAPAN OPERATION, 23–25 JANUARY 1942

On 20 January, following the sighting of a Japanese invasion force approaching Balikpapan, Adm. Glassford left Timor with two American light cruisers and six destroyers. However, the next day the cruiser USS *Boise* struck a reef in the Sape Strait, and was escorted away for repairs, while Glassford's other cruiser *Marblehead* was plagued by engine problems. Still, on 22 January, Glassford sent Destroyer Division 59's (DesDiv 59) four destroyers north to attack the enemy transports off Balikpapan, while *Marblehead* and an escorting destroyer headed to a rendezvous point south of the target. Cdr Talbot, leading DesDiv 59 slowly skirted the Celebes coast, before striking across the Strait towards Balikpapan on the evening of 24 January. The attackers were lucky – Adm. Nishimura's escort force had put to sea a few hours earlier to hunt for Dutch submarines. So Talbot had a clear run, sinking three transports and damaging two more. The high-speed withdrawal led to a rendezvous with *Marblehead* soon after dawn, and Glassford's force withdrew across the Java Sea to Sourabaya. It was arguably ABDA's only successful operation, and indeed the attack on the Japanese transport fleet anchored off Balikpapan early on 25 January demonstrated ABDA's resolve to defend its theatre of operations. However, it failed to derail or even slow down the Japanese conquest of the East Indies.

Japanese transports
Balikpapan
ASW search by Adm. Nishimura's escorts (night 24/25 Jan)
04.30/25
Midnight/ 24/25
MAKASSAR STRAIT
Destroyer Retirement
DUTCH BORNEO
Rendezvous 08.00/25
CELEBES
19.30/24
Group Withdrawal
To Sourabaya
JAVA SEA
Makassar
16.32/23
USS Marblehead
FLORES SEA
US destroyers
Lombok Strait
BALI
LOMBOK
Alas Strait
Sape Strait
SUMBAWA

guardship, the Dutch minesweeper HNLMS *Prins van Oranje* was sunk by the destroyer IJNS *Yamakaze*, supported by a patrol boat, No. 38. Later that morning, Japan officially declared war against the Netherlands. Supporting the invasion were aircraft of the 21st Naval Air Flotilla, based at Davao in the Philippines. By the end of 12 January, the remains of the small Dutch garrison on Tarakan surrendered to the Japanese. However, two Japanese minesweepers were lost there, to Dutch-laid mines.

The Second Japanese invasion force appeared off Menado to the north-east of Celebes before dawn on 11 January. There, eight transports were protected by R. Adm. Tanaka's 2nd Destroyer Squadron, with a light cruiser, ten destroyers and two seaplane carriers. There the landings began at 0400hrs, and the Dutch defenders were quickly ejected from the town. So too was its airfield, and the 21st Air Flotilla immediately began relocating there, which greatly extended its reach to the south. On the same day, landings were made near Jesselton in British North Borneo, to complete the conquests that began on 23 December and 6 January, following landings in Sarawak and Brunei.

Then, on 21 January, the Japanese continued their drive south in Dutch Borneo, when V. Adm. Taskahashi's Central Invasion Group moved on from Tarakan to Balikpapan, 270nm to the south. A total of 18 transports left Tarakan at 1100hrs on 21 January, escorted by R. Adm. Hirosi's 11 destroyers and 2 light cruisers, and covered by a distant covering force of heavy cruisers and more destroyers. The Central Invasion Group arrived off Balikpapan late on 23 January, and the assault force went ashore at 2130hrs. One of the transport, the *Nana Maru*, was sunk in a bombing raid, while the Dutch submarine *K-17* sank another in the Makassar Strait. That prompted most of the escorts to put to sea, to hunt for the submarine, leaving the transport ships largely undefended as they lay at anchor off the port.

Under ABDA's division of forces, the defence of the Makassar Strait was largely the responsibility of Adm. Glassford. On 20 January, his all-American force was anchored in Kupang Bay in Timor. *Houston* and several destroyers were away on escort duty, but Glassford still had the light cruisers *Boise* and

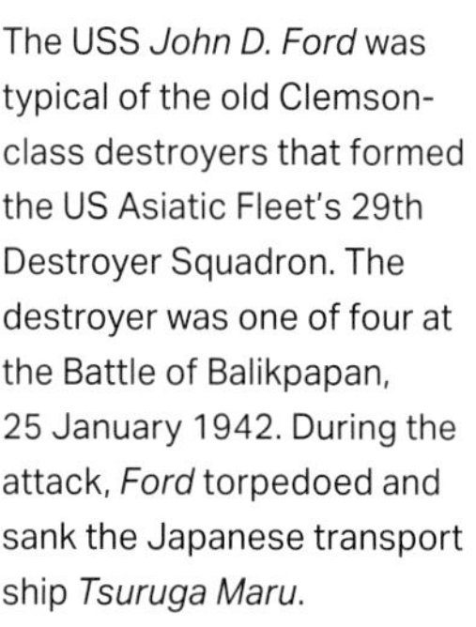

The USS *John D. Ford* was typical of the old Clemson-class destroyers that formed the US Asiatic Fleet's 29th Destroyer Squadron. The destroyer was one of four at the Battle of Balikpapan, 25 January 1942. During the attack, *Ford* torpedoed and sank the Japanese transport ship *Tsuruga Maru*.

The old Clemson-class destroyer USS *Parrott*, laying down a smokescreen using funnel smoke. *Parrott* took part in the Battle of Balikpapan, but was on escort duty for much of February, and so missed the debacle in the Java Sea. *Parrott* survived the campaign, and remained in service throughout the war.

Marblehead and six destroyers at hand. He led these ships to sea, but progress was slowed by *Marblehead*, the faulty turbine of which limited the force's speed to 15kts. The following day, 21 January, Glassford's flagship *Boise* ran aground on an uncharted rock in the Sape Strait, between the East Indies islands of Sumbawa and Flores, which ripped a hole in the cruiser's hull 120ft long. So, after the admiral had shifted to *Marblehead* on 22 January, *Boise*, with the destroyer *Pillsbury* as escort, was sent off to Tjilatjap in Java, on the first leg of a journey that would lead to repairs in Bombay.

Glassford then decided that *Marblehead*'s engine problems would delay his counter-attack. So, he detached the destroyer flotilla, retaining one of them, the destroyer *Bulmer*, before sending the flotilla north on its own under the command of Cdr. Talbot of the *John D. Ford*. Then he took *Marblehead* off across the Java Sea, accompanied by the destroyer *Bulmer* to take up a covering position off the south-east coast of Borneo. This meant the attack force was reduced to just four obsolete destroyers (*John D. Ford*, *Pope*, *Parrott* and

THE BATTLE OF BALIKPAPAN, SATURDAY 24 JANUARY 1942

On the evening of 23 January, a Japanese invasion fleet arrived off the port of Balikpapan in Dutch Borneo. Maj. Gen. Sakaguchi's invasion force disembarked, and a two-day battle against the Dutch defenders ensued. Balikpapan contained a major oil refinery, and this was soon burning fiercely, covering the anchorage in a thick cloud of oily black smoke. That evening the bulk of R. Adm. Nishimura's fleet left the anchorage, to hunt for Dutch warships. Only four small patrol boats and minesweepers remained to protect the 16 transports. Meanwhile, off Timor, Adm. Hart, commanding the US Navy's Asiatic Squadron, decided to attack the transports.

Consequently, at around 0245hrs on Saturday morning, Cdr Talbot's force of four aged US Navy destroyers approached the anchorage off Balikpapan. It was a moonless night, and the darkness and dense smoke made visibility difficult. Still, staying in line astern, with Talbot's USS *John D. Ford* in the lead, his destroyers began their attack. For the next hour, they criss-crossed the anchorage, firing their guns and launching torpedoes at any targets they encountered. Their assault lasted a little over an hour. This plate shows the last few minutes of the attack, at 0347hrs, as the *Ford* launches its last torpedo at the transport *Tsuraga Maru* on the Americans' port beam, while all four destroyers fire their main batteries of 4in guns. Once all the torpedoes were expended, Talbot led his destroyers back out to sea, leaving five transports sunk and two more, as well as a patrol ship, badly damaged. This daring action was a rare success for ABDA forces during the campaign.

Paul Jones), under the command of Cdr Talbot of the *Ford*. They entered the Makassar Strait in the late afternoon of 23 January and arrived off Balikpapan an hour after sunset. In fact, Glassford made a vain effort to join them, heading north into the Java Sea with *Marblehead* and *Bulmer*, to provide what support he could to Talbot's destroyer flotilla.

Talbot's instructions were to attack with torpedoes first. His captains were to avoid opening fire with the destroyers' guns until all torpedoes had been expended. He finished by adding: '*Use initiative and determination*.' He approached the anchorage with his destroyers in line astern, with *Ford* in the lead, making 27kts. Talbot was lucky that most of the Japanese warships were at sea. It also helped that the transport ships were silhouetted by the orange flames lighting up the bay, as the Balikpapan oil refinery was on fire. Although this action has been called a battle, mainly as it was the first time the US Navy had fought a surface action since 1898, it was more of a one-sided turkey shoot. The American destroyers approached from the south-east, and at 0246hrs on 24 January they were within torpedo range.

Parrott launched first at 0256hrs, but all eight torpedoes missed their mark. *Ford* and *Paul Jones* both fired a single torpedo at an unidentified target, probably a patrol boat, but missed the vessel. Talbot then led his destroyers around in a loop, to approach the lines of transports from another angle. *Parrott* launched three more torpedoes, and this time, at 0300hrs, one struck the transport *Sumanura Maru*, which blew up. A few minutes later, torpedoes from *Paul Jones* and *Pope* sunk another, the *Tatsukami Maru*, as Talbot's destroyers settled on their reciprocal course. Then, as Talbot turned west, they wrecked a Japanese patrol boat, *PC-37*, to port, before looping round again to steam northwards through the middle of the anchorage. However, *Pope* and *Parrott* had by then used up all their torpedoes.

They passed the burning hulk of the *Nana Maru*, wrecked in an earlier air attack, and passed between two more transports, *Tsuruga Maru* to port and *Asahi Maru* to starboard. *Ford* and *Paul Jones* launched three torpedoes between them at *Tsuruga Maru*, and one from *Paul Jones* hit the ship, which began to sink. At 0347hrs, *Ford* was hit by gunfire from the *Asahi Maru*, so all destroyers returned fire, riddling the transport. Then Talbot ordered them to break off the action, with *Ford* turning to port and the rest to starboard. However, by 0350hrs they'd reformed just south of the Japanese anchorage, and Talbot led them away into the darkness of the Makassar Strait, leaving a scene of chaos and confusion behind him. By dawn they spotted *Marblehead* and *Bulmer*, and the American ships sped south, before Japanese aircraft could find them. The tally was three transports sunk and a patrol boat. While impressive, it did nothing to stop the Japanese landing or impede the speed of the enemy's advance through the Dutch East Indies.

Flores Sea

By 3 February, R. Adm. Doorman, commanding ABDA's Striking Force, had managed to assemble part of his squadron in Bounder Roads, on the south side of Madura Island, to the east of the Javanese port of Sourabaya. The British contingent was still at sea escorting shipping, but the American and Dutch contingents were available. That day, the Japanese launched a heavy air attack on the port, and the Allied warships were spotted, lying in the roads as the Japanese aircraft passed over Madura to reach Sourabaya. By then, the Japanese had landed at Kandari, on the south-eastern arm of Celebes, and had moved much of the 21st Naval Air Flotilla there to extend its range. This should have warned Doorman that the enemy would have enjoyed air superiority over the intervening Flores Sea.

However, when word reached him that a Japanese invasion force with 20 transports had just passed through the Makassar Strait, and appeared to be approaching Makassar, in the south-west end of Celebes, he led his Striking Force into the Flores Sea, in an attempt to intercept it. Doorman flew his flag in *De Ruyter*, which was accompanied by a second Dutch light cruiser, *Tromp*, as well as the US cruisers *Houston* and *Marblehead*, four American destroyers (*Barker*, *Bulmer*, *John D. Edwards* and *Stewart*) and three Dutch ones (*Banckert*, *Piet Hein* and *Van Ghent*). The cruisers were formed up in line astern of the flagship, with the Dutch destroyers in a similar column to port, and the American ones to starboard.

Four groups of large Japanese bombers were detected approaching from the east at 0949hrs. The first sighting was made by lookouts aboard *Houston*, rather than by radar. These were 27 Mitsubishi Mi-G4M1 'Betty' twin-engined bombers of Kanoya Air Groups, which circled overhead at 14,000ft, keeping just out of AA range while they selected their target. Doorman sent a signal to Sourabaya, saying simply 'Send Fighters!', but the chances of this happening were slim. So, he ordered his ships to break formation and disperse, scattering at high speed, to force the attackers to split into smaller groups. At that time, the value of close formation air defence was still largely undiscovered. *Houston* even tried to launch her floatplanes, but only one was catapulted off before the bombers made their move.

At 0953hrs, the bombers were seen to break up into groups and ignoring the destroyers each of the four formations concentrated on the Allied cruisers. A minute later, nine bombers targeted *Marblehead*. Capt. Robinson turned hard, but the bombers passed overhead without dropping their bombs – they were testing his ship's AA defences. Meanwhile, *Houston* fired at approaching bombers with the 5in battery, with no effect; afterwards, Capt. Rooks reckoned the shells were defective. The nine bombers made a second pass at *Marblehead*, so Robinson turned again, but this turned out to be another feint. Then another newly arrived Betty from the Takao Air Group came in for pass, and this time they kept coming. The bombs were dropped from 14,000ft, and

Capt. Albert H. Rooks commanded HMS *Houston* during the campaign and fought his ship with courage and professionalism. However, together with most of his men, the 50-year-old veteran officer was lost when *Houston* was sunk at the Battle of Sunda Strait on 1 March. He was later posthumously awarded the Medal of Honor for his gallantry and distinguished service.

for a third time Robinson turned his ship, avoiding any direct hit. One of the bombers was hit and crashed into the sea, possibly hit by fire from *De Ruyter*.

Then, at 1019hrs, another attack approached the two American cruisers, with eight to nine attacking each ship. At the last moment, Capt. Rooks turned hard to port, and the bombs missed *Houston*. The only casualty was the ship's AA director, which became jammed during the tight turn. However, there were several near misses, and the crew described how some of these near misses bucked the cruiser about in the water like a toy. By then, yet more bombers had arrived – 24 Mitsubishi G3M 'Nell' twin-engined bombers of the 1st Air Group.

The first 'V-shaped' flight of nine of these headed for *Marblehead*. At 1027hrs, as the ship turned hard, a 250kg semi-armour-piercing (SAP) bomb struck the cruiser forward and exploded below decks. The blast wrecked the sick bay and wardroom, and caused devastation within the cruiser. Fires erupted through the blast hole in the deck. A second hit struck the cruiser's quarterdeck, jamming the rudder. The ship was turning hard to port when the bomb detonated, and so the ship continued to turn in circles, trailing oil as it went. Another narrow miss buckled the bow plates of *Marblehead*, and the old cruiser began taking on water and listing ten degrees to starboard. It looked like the end for *Marblehead*, but when *Tromp* approached and Capt. De Meester offered to take off the crew, Robinson waved the Dutch ship away. He was confident his damage-control parties could keep *Marblehead* afloat. He was right. By 1100hrs, his crew had the fire under control.

USS *Marblehead*, pictured alongside the quay in Tjilatjap in Java, showing the impact of a Japanese 138.5lb (62.8kg) bomb hit on the elderly light cruiser's stern. The ship would have been sunk were it not for the efforts of the ship's damage control teams. After being patched up there, *Marblehead* was then sent to Ceylon and finally New York for repairs.

Four minutes later, another attacking formation headed towards *Marblehead*, but this proved to be another feint – the real attack was on *Houston*. This dummy was followed by a real one at 1117hrs, but the bombers of 1st Air Group hadn't reckoned with Capt. Rooks' superb ship-handling. The cruiser weaved its way through the bomb splashes, many of which fell close by, and showered the cruiser with spray and shrapnel, but no real damage was done. Then, ten minutes later, the next wave of bombers appeared. This time it was the Dutch flagship that was the target. *De Ruyter* was straddled, but somehow Capt. Lacomblé missed the bombs, although a near-miss put his Hazemeyer fire control director out of action.

By 1130hrs, Capt. Rooks saw another bomber formation lining up for an attack on *Marblehead* – no doubt trying to finish the battered cruiser off. He turned *Houston* to close the distance between the two cruisers, to increase the effectiveness of their joint air defences. It might have worked, had the Japanese not switched targets at the last minute and turned towards *Houston*. By then, Rooks had developed a method of lying on his back, following the bombers through his binoculars, to judge when to start his ship's turn. At 1140hrs, seeing the aircraft approach from port, Rooks gave the order, but this time he misjudged it. A group of the bombers had guessed the American ship's move, and their bombs straddled the fast-turning cruiser.

One of them struck the top of the heavy cruiser's after turret, the guns of which were trained to port, and detonated on the turret's side, killing the gun crew and blowing a hole in the deck beside it. This blast ignited powder bags in the handling room and started a major fire. It was only quick thinking by the surviving crew that prevented this spreading to the magazine. By then, the last of the bombers had departed, leaving the crew of *Houston* and *Marblehead* to deal with the damage. In all, 48 of *Houston*'s crew were killed and 20 more wounded, while aboard *Marblehead* 15 were killed and another 34 wounded, most of them seriously. ABDA Striking Force had taken a serious beating. So at 1225hrs, Doorman ordered his squadron to abandon the mission and to return to Sourabaya, where, if the Japanese bombers hadn't wrecked everything, there were repair facilities to hand. However, at 1415hrs, following reports from *Houston* and *Marblehead*, Doorman ordered them to detach, and head through the Lombok Strait to Tjilatjap, on Java's south coast. The port had, so far, been spared by the Japanese bombers, and had repair facilities which might help the American crews patch up their ships.

Banka

After the Flores Sea incident, *Houston* put into Sourabaya for repairs, while *Marblehead* went to the smaller port of Tjilatjap. However, the heavy cruiser's after turret would be out of action until it could be repaired in an American shipyard. Adm. Hart decided to keep *Houston* anyway, as the ship was too useful, but he ordered *Marblehead* to head to Colombo in Ceylon after temporary repairs were complete, and then proceed on to New York, after being made seaworthy in the British base. The effectiveness of ABDA Striking Force had

The heavy cruiser HMS *Exeter*, under attack from Japanese aircraft from IJNS *Ryujo* during the morning of 15 February, off Banka Island to the east of Sumatra. Hidden by the bomb splashes is the Australian light cruiser HMAS *Hobart*, while on the right is an unidentified Dutch destroyer. This ABDA sortie was called off shortly after, and *Exeter* returned safely to Java.

been reduced, but it was still powerful enough to do some damage to the Japanese. As the Japanese reached the outskirts of Singapore, a Japanese invasion force was sighted to the south-east of Celebes. The following day it arrived off Makassar, and quickly seized control of the town. This allowed the Japanese to move their aircraft even closer to Java.

Also on 9 February, a large Japanese force was sighted in the South China Sea, heading south from Cam Ranh Bay in Indochina. It was V. Adm. Ozawa's Western Invasion Group, made up of five heavy cruisers, including his flagship *Chokai*, the light carrier *Ryujo* and a flotilla of six destroyers. The carrier had 27 aircraft embarked: 12 Mitsubishi A5M 'Claude' fighters, the forerunner of the 'Zero', and 15 Nakajima B5N 'Kate' torpedo bombers. By 11 February, *Ryujo* had been joined by R. Adm. Hashimoto's Advanced Echelon of eight transports, escorted by five destroyers and seven smaller warships. The following day, another force of 17 transports, a light cruiser, two destroyers and five smaller warships arrived. It was clear that another major invasion was under way.

So, on 12 February, Doorman gathered together five cruisers and ten destroyers, and headed towards Oosthaven (now Bandar Lampung) in the south-eastern corner of Sumatra. A collision in dense fog saw *De Ruyter* collide with the destroyer USS *Whipple*, which had to return to Tjilatjap with a badly bent bow. On 14 February, Doorman's squadron passed through the Sunda Strait, heading for Banka Island (now Bangka Island), off the east coast of Sumatra. However, at 0520hrs on 14 February, while transiting the passage between Banka and the smaller island of Billiton (now Belitung) to the east, the Dutch destroyer *Van Ghent* ran aground on the Bamidjo Reef. The ship was wrecked, so leaving the destroyer *Banckert* behind to rescue the crew, Doorman pressed on, to take up position to the north-east of Banka. Altogether it was an unfortunate start to ABDA Striking Force's second offensive sweep.

ABDA STRIKING FORCE'S AIR DEFENCE: SCATTERING VS CLOSE FORMATION

In the Flores Sea, on the morning of 4 February, when ABDA Striking Force came under heavy air attack, the formation followed the orders issued by V. Adm. Doorman. The Dutch commander adopted early-war procedures, which called on the striking force's warships to scatter, to break up the attacking air formations approaching at 14,000ft. So, as the ABDA warships dispersed, it was a case of each ship for itself. As a result, the three waves of Japanese bombers concentrated on the largest targets, and *De Ruyter*, *Houston* and *Marblehead* were all damaged. Of these, *Houston*'s damage was the most serious, as the American cruiser's after triple 8in turret was put out of action for the remainder of the campaign.

In its next daytime sortie into the Java Sea on 15 February, when attacked off Banka Island, thanks to British and Australian pressure, Doorman adopted a closed formation, of the kind which bitter experience had taught the Royal Navy was far more effective. As a result, instead of each ship defending itself, now the whole formation provided mutual protection, which greatly increased its chances of deterring an attack or shooting down an enemy aircraft.

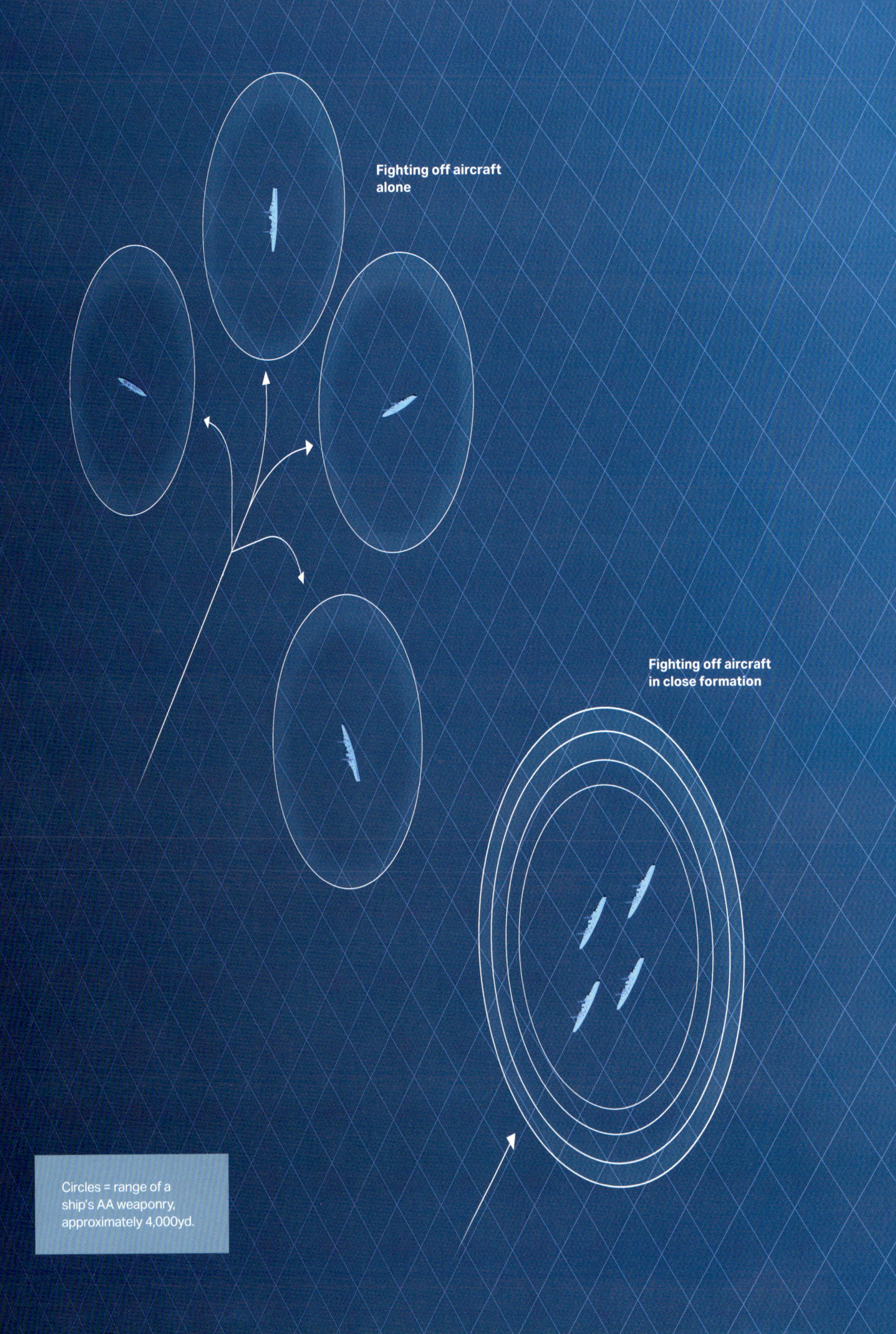
Fighting off aircraft
alone
Fighting off aircraft
in close formation
Circles = range of a
ship's AA weaponry,
approximately 4,000yd.

The Dutch light cruiser *Java*, under air attack off Banka Island, to the east of Sumatra, on 15 February. Surprisingly, despite numerous attacks on the cruiser, Java didn't receive any direct hits, and the only damage was from splinters from near misses exploding close to the ship's hull. *Java* though, would be sunk in action less than two weeks later.

Intelligence reports suggested that the Japanese were heading for Sumatra, with a likely landing area around the marshy mouth of the Musi River, which led to Palembang, 45 miles to the south-west. This city was home to two oil refineries and the largest oil-producing centre in all of the East Indies, so it made sense that the Japanese were attempting to capture it. Doorman decided to turn around and loop clockwise around Banka, then fall on the unsuspecting Japanese transport fleet as it lay at anchor off the river mouth. However, Japanese reconnaissance planes had already spotted the Allied force. So, while V. Adm. Ozawa held his transports back, he used *Ryujo* to launch air strikes on the ABDA formation, as it cruised off Banka. They were joined by groups of the 21st Naval Air Flotilla; from 1020hrs, for eight hours, Doorman's ships were subjected to a seemingly endless succession of naval air strikes.

This time the ABDA ships remained concentrated, which helped create a heavy fire to deter the attackers. The warships also used speed and manoeuvrability to avoid the rain of bombs. It helped that the Japanese tended to bomb from a high altitude. However, during an attack by 23 Mitsubishi G3M2 Nell bombers from Genzan Air Group based at Kuching in Sarawak, the destroyers USS *Barker* and USS *Bulmer* both sustained hull damage from near misses, which caused flooding. At 1242hrs Doorman had had enough of these attacks and ordered his Striking Force to withdraw to the south-east. Still, the air attacks continued, small ones from *Ryujo*, and larger ones from land-based formations. The last one at 1830hrs was carried out by 17 Betty bombers of the veteran Kanoya Air Group, flying from Saigon in Indochina, some 800nm and a five-hour flight away. These veterans of the destruction of Force Z though, had no luck against the ABDA formation.

This abortive operation achieved nothing, apart from the loss of *Van Ghent* and damage to three American destroyers, which needed repairs before they could resume operations. Meanwhile, the Japanese landing went ahead, and Palembang and its refineries duly fell to them on 15 February. That same day, Singapore also fell to the Japanese, and over 85,000 British and Commonwealth troops were captured. It was a disaster for the British, but it also marked the end for ABDA too. With Singapore by then in Japanese hands, and Sumatra in the process of being overrun, the Malay Barrier had been demolished. So, all ABDA could do was to hold on to Java and the remaining islands of the Dutch East Indies for as long as it could, while hoping for a change of fortune.

Badung Strait

By then, all of Java was well within range of Japanese bombers, and regular bombing raids were clearly designed to soften up the island's defences, before the launch of a large-scale amphibious invasion. The Japanese also conducted regular anti-shipping sweeps over the Java Sea, and on 17 February the Dutch destroyer *Van Nes* was sunk in an air attack off Billiton, carried out by aircraft from *Ryujo*. At the time, *Van Nes* was escorting a merchant ship to Java, crowded with Dutch refugees from Billiton. Both ships were sunk, with the loss of 70 of the destroyer's crew and 249 civilians. Most of these attacks reduced the ability of the Dutch naval bases in Java to support ABDA's warships, and placed them at risk of suffering damage or loss.

On 18 February, during a raid on Sourabaya, a bomb dropped by a Betty from the Takao Air Group landed on top of the Dutch submarine *K-7*, which had submerged to avoid being hit. One struck it anyway, and all of the stricken boat's crew died when it refused to surface, and all rescue attempts proved abortive. Another bomb damaged the Dutch destroyer *Banckert*. The following day, the Allies were ready for the raid and had assembled all available fighters over the port. It didn't do much good though, as in the major aerial dogfight that followed, the more modern Japanese Zeros shot down 40 Dutch and American fighters, for the loss of one fighter of their own. That same day, Adm. Nagumo's Carrier Force, with its Pearl Harbor veterans embarked, launched an air attack on Darwin, from a flying-off position east of Timor. The 242 fighters and bombers hadn't been detected, and at 0920hrs the mass raid took the Australian port by surprise. In all, some 14 vessels were sunk or run aground, one of which was the destroyer USS *Peary*, and another 25 damaged, including the destroyer USS *William B. Preston*.

That same evening, the Japanese landed near Sanur on the east coast of Bali. This was less than 40 miles to the east of Java, and meant that ABDA Striking Force was on hand to intervene. Doorman's warships were scattered between several Javanese anchorages, so coordinating a joint attack proved impossible. At 2225hrs that evening, the first ABDA group rounded Cape Tafel (Tafelhoek) on

Throughout the campaign, the Dutch light cruiser HNLMS *De Ruyter* served as the flagship of R. Adm. Doorman, commander of ABDA's Striking Force. Built in the 1930s, the cruiser was relatively small and lightly armed, compared to other modern 6in cruisers, but it was still the most powerful Dutch warship in the East Indies.

the south-eastern corner of the island. This force was led by Doorman himself, having left Tjilatjap that afternoon. His flagship *De Ruyter* was followed by *Java* and five destroyers (*Piet Hein*, *Evertsen*, *John D. Ford*, *Pope* and *Edsall*) followed the cruisers in line astern. Doorman's intention was to use speed and surprise to overwhelm the enemy. Instead, ABDA Striking Force narrowly avoided disaster.

On rounding the headland, Doorman turned to the north-east and entered the Badung Strait, keeping about three miles offshore. It was a dark, moonless night, with low clouds, which made visibility difficult. At 2325hrs, lookouts aboard Java sighted three shapes ahead, which were illuminated using searchlights. The anchorage was almost devoid of ships. What they'd spotted was the damaged transport ship *Sasago Maru*, attended by two destroyers, the *Asashio* and *Oshio*. Java opened up on *Asashio* at a range of just over a mile. The Japanese quickly got under way, while replying with their own guns. They were commanded by Capt. Abe Toshio of *Oshio*, who led the two destroyers towards the east, and so 'crossed the T' of the approaching Allies. The Japanese targeted *Java*, aiming at the searchlights, and their guns scored several hits. *Oshio* then switched fire to *De Ruyter*, but in the pitch darkness neither ship managed to hit the other.

Doorman ordered starshells to be fired, to help guide the destroyers, which had lagged a few miles behind the cruisers. The leading one, *Piet Hein*, spotted ships to port, and launched five torpedoes, which all missed. The two leading US destroyers, *Ford* and *Pope*, also launched torpedo salvos, with no better result, although *Pope* later claimed a hit on a transport ship. These ships were the *Sasago Maru* and the *Asashio*, which had been left behind when the Dutch cruisers had sped past, duelling with *Oshio*. In the melee that followed *Asashio* took on all three destroyers, firing guns and launching torpedoes. At 2340hrs, one of the torpedoes struck *Piet Hein*, and following a huge explosion the shattered destroyer began sinking. *Asashio* then sped past at point-blank range, firing into the wreck.

At that point, Cdr Parker of *Parrott* led the American destroyers in a loop, and pursued *Asashio*, which had been joined by *Oshio*. A running gunnery duel

The design of the Dutch light cruiser HNLMS *Java* was based on World War I German light cruisers, and entered service in 1921. The ship was modified slightly in the 1930s, but generally the design compared unfavourably with more modern cruisers such as *De Ruyter*.

towards the south-east followed, but when the Japanese gunnery proved much more accurate, Parker broke off the fight, with *Pope* launching a salvo of five torpedoes to screen the withdrawal. Not only did these not hit anything, but the two Japanese destroyers turned and pursued the Americans. Minutes later, a Japanese searchlight picked out *Ford*, and the destroyer was fired at from close range, but was unscathed. Parker ordered a smoke screen to be laid to hide his destroyers and then he turned towards the south to buy time in order to regroup. Instead, *Asashio* and *Oshio* turned to follow, resulting in another exchange of fire, with the two sides steering parallel courses, until the Americans withdrew behind another smoke screen, and headed back to Tjilatjap.

Meanwhile, the two Dutch cruisers had been searching for the transport fleet, and on finding it gone, Doorman ordered *Java* to follow the flagship back to Sourabaya. Capt. Abe led his two destroyers back to rejoin the damaged transport ship. By midnight, it seemed that the battle was over. However, at 0115hrs, the Allied second wave appeared – the cruiser *Tromp* and the US destroyers *Stewart*, *Parrott*, *John D. Edwards* and *Pillsbury*. Once in Badung Strait, they spotted signalling lights ahead, which they took to be enemy warships. A total of 15 torpedoes were launched at the still unseen enemy, but these all failed to hit anything.

Then, two Japanese destroyers appeared out of the darkness to port, guns blazing. At 0146hrs, *Stewart*, revealed by its own searchlights, was hit in the steering compartments, partially disabling the old destroyer. More torpedoes were launched at the two Japanese destroyers, but again they either missed or malfunctioned. The running gunfight continued for some minutes before the four remaining American destroyers could break off the action. At that point, at around 0200hrs, *Tromp* appeared, and battled the two enemy destroyers at close range, hitting them both with 6in shells. *Tromp* though, was hit 11 times, causing damage to the cruiser's fire control and gunnery director equipment. Then contact was lost, and *Tromp* followed the destroyers, breaking off the engagement.

However, the battle wasn't quite over. At the same time, two more Japanese destroyers arrived in the area from the north – *Arashio* and *Michishio*. Twenty minutes later, they made contact with the US destroyers, firing at *Stewart* and *John D. Edwards*. This time it was the Japanese destroyer that came off worse; it was badly damaged and stopped in the water. However, the Americans lost sight of the crippled destroyer in the dark, and *Michishio* was eventually towed to Makassar by *Arashio*, where emergency repairs were made. Finally, at 0245hrs, seven Dutch motor torpedo boats entered the Badung Strait, but finding nothing to attack, they returned to Sourabaya.

This marked the end of a confused night action, fought in pitch darkness, in which two Japanese destroyers had effectively held ABDA Striking Force at bay, sinking a destroyer and damaging another, as well as the cruiser *Tromp*. In return, the Allies had crippled a Japanese destroyer and damaged two more.

However, it made no difference to the battle for Bali. The island had already fallen, and by the morning of 20 February, the Tainan Air Group had arrived at Denpasar airfield there. This meant that Japanese strike aircraft were based less than 200 miles from Sourabaya. The Japanese choke hold around Java was tightening. The following day, this was tightened further when the Japanese landed at Timor, at the eastern end of the island chain, to tighten the grip, and sever safe sea communications between Java and Darwin. Although ABDA's warships would fight on, save for Java, the island chain which had made up the Malay Barrier was in enemy hands.

Java Sea

It was inevitable that the next Japanese target would be Java. Adm. Helfrich, who had taken command of ABDA Float from Adm. Hart, took solace in the fact that the Sunda and Bali Straits were still open, and so in theory Java could still be supplied and reinforced. In truth, the situation was hopeless. Even Gen. Wavell realized this, and felt continued Allied resistance was merely a way of showing solidarity with the Dutch more than anything else. Had he known it, the final blow was already on its way. V. Adm. Takahashi's Java Invasion Group had been divided into Eastern and Western forces, with 41 and 52 transport ships respectively. Both were screened by substantial destroyer groups and further protected by Covering Groups of cruisers and more destroyers.

In Java, an air of defeat hung over the island. Still, V. Adm. Helfrich and R. Adm. Doorman were determined to fight on, despite the gradual whittling down of the Allied squadron to mishaps or enemy bombs. The destroyers *Stewart* and *Banckert* were wrecked while in Sourabaya, *Whipple* and *Edsall* were out of action until repaired, *Pillsbury* and *Parrott* needed repairing, while *Barker* and *Bulmer* both needed a complete mechanical overhaul, so they were sent off to Australia. The Dutch yards did what they could, but progress was slow. Even the operational ships were in poor shape, and short of torpedoes, stores and ordnance.

This is the last photograph of the Australian light cruiser HMAS *Perth*, taken on the afternoon of 28 February, before *Perth* and *Houston* made their doomed attempt to reach the Sunda Strait. While the starboard side of the cruiser still bore a splinter-pattern camouflage, this port side appears to have been overpainted in mid-grey, in an unfinished attempt to appear less conspicuous.

On 21 February, Helfrich gathered a handful of warships in Tanjong Priok, the port serving Batavia, and grandly named these the Western Striking Force. These included the Australian light cruiser *Hobart*, and the obsolete British light cruisers *Danae* and *Dragon*, supported by a pair of elderly British destroyers, *Scout* and *Tenedos*, and the more modern Dutch destroyer *Evertsen*. This virtually useless force was charged with protecting the western approaches to Java. By 25 February, when ABDA Command was broken into its constituent elements, it was tentatively redesignated ABDA Area, although it lacked central leadership. In truth, with a shrinking naval force and only 15 operational fighters, there was little the Allied commanders in Java could do.

It was unfortunate that this restructuring coincided with the arrival of the Japanese. At that time, the Western Invasion Force was in the South China Sea, between Malaya and Borneo, while south of Java, Adm. Kondo's battlefleet, accompanied by Adm. Nagumo's Carrier Strike Force, was cutting off any line of retreat from Java. In the Java Sea, south of Borneo, the Eastern Invasion Force was biding its time, waiting for its moment, at the southern end of the Makassar Strait. Whatever Adm. Doorman did, there was no chance of escaping the impending blow.

On 26 February, Helfrich ordered the Western Striking Force to sea, to patrol around Banka, and provide warning of any attack. There was no sign of a Japanese invasion force, and so after being bombed, and running short of fuel, Capt. Howden of *Hobart* led his force back to Tanjong Priok. He was lucky. Later that day, Allied aircraft spotted an invasion force of 30 transports and their escorts south of Banka heading towards the Sunda Strait. So, Helfrich reluctantly ordered the entire force, save *Evertsen*, to refuel, then escape through the Strait, and make for the safety of Ceylon, thus avoiding a wasteful sacrifice. Meanwhile, Helfrich ordered *Exeter*, *Perth* and the three remaining British destroyers to Tanjong Priok to join Doorman's hastily re-assembled Striking Force.

The Dutch destroyer HNLMS *Kortenaer* was a Van Ghent-class destroyer, a modified version of the British A class, and completed in 1927. *Kortenaer* was sunk at the Battle of the Java Sea, while the destroyer's three sister ships *Van Ghent*, *Piet Hein* and *Evertsen* were also lost during the campaign.

Hopes of better air cover died when the seaplane carrier USS *Langley* was sunk by Japanese aircraft 50 miles from Tjilatjap. *Langley* was carrying P-40 fighters to provide air cover for Doorman. So, with the Japanese closing in, Doorman would have to try and stop the enemy without any substantial air cover. At 1830hrs on Thursday 26 February, Doorman put to sea in *De Ruyter*, accompanied by *Exeter*, *Houston*, *Java*, *Perth* and nine destroyers. The intention was a coastal sweep as far west as Madura Island near Sourabaya. This was aborted at 1427hrs on Friday, when word reached Doorman that a Japanese invasion fleet was off Bawean Island, 80 miles north of Sourabaya. The Striking Force headed off to intercept the enemy, but Doorman had no clear idea of how strong this enemy force was.

In fact, R. Adm. Nishimura's invasion force was made up of 41 transport ships, escorted by 13 destroyers in two flotillas, led by Nishimura's flagship, the light cruiser *Naka*, and accompanied by another light cruiser, *Jintsu*. Some 20 miles behind Nishimura was R. Adm. Takagi with the heavy cruisers *Nachi* and *Haguro* and two more destroyers. Doorman didn't realize it, but in effect he was sailing into a trap. Worse still, the Japanese had substantial air cover, while Doorman didn't.

At 1612hrs, lookouts aboard the destroyer *Electra* sighted an enemy cruiser and a destroyer 14 miles to the north-west. At the time, ABDA Striking Force was 20 miles off the Java coast. The enemy cruiser was *Jintsu*, which opened fire, and *Electra* and *Jupiter* replied. Then the two Japanese heavy cruisers appeared to the north and opened fire too. The 2nd Destroyer Flotilla then closed with the British destroyers.

A COMPARISON OF TORPEDO CAPABILITIES: ABDA AND THE JAPANESE NAVY

When the campaign began, apart from the guidance problems which plagued American-built 21in Mark 14 torpedoes, and despite ongoing supply and maintenance problems, ABDA's naval commanders felt they were reasonably well equipped with torpedoes. Then, during the opening phase of the Battle of the Java Sea, any confidence was shattered. The range and effectiveness of the Imperial Japanese Navy's 24in Type 93 Long Lance torpedoes came as a shock. Until then, their naval tactics had been built around the notion that the maximum range of a torpedo was around 7,000–9,000yds – around four nautical miles. That's why the realization that the Japanese torpedo was both faster and had a range roughly five times greater came as a major shock.

When a Type 93 torpedo did hit its target, it was found that it had a warhead which was significantly larger than its Allied counterparts. So, the chance of the torpedo inflicting crippling damage was significantly greater. The final element was numbers. At the Java Sea, discounting the four old American destroyers which had run out of torpedoes, the Japanese had 154 24in torpedoes at their disposal, while ABDA had 54 21in ones – a ratio of almost three to one. At the Battle of the Sunda Strait, the numbers were even more skewed in Japan's favour, with 110 torpedoes to 14 Allied ones – a ratio of almost eight to one.

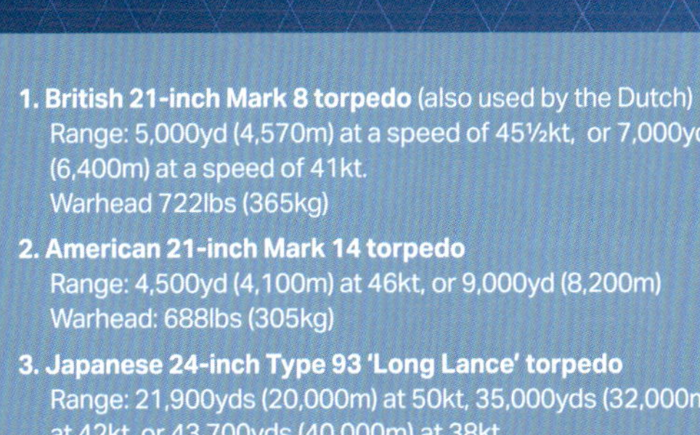

1. **British 21-inch Mark 8 torpedo** (also used by the Dutch)
   Range: 5,000yd (4,570m) at a speed of 45½kt, or 7,000yd (6,400m) at a speed of 41kt.
   Warhead 722lbs (365kg)
2. **American 21-inch Mark 14 torpedo**
   Range: 4,500yd (4,100m) at 46kt, or 9,000yd (8,200m)
   Warhead: 688lbs (305kg)
3. **Japanese 24-inch Type 93 'Long Lance' torpedo**
   Range: 21,900yds (20,000m) at 50kt, 35,000yds (32,000m) at 42kt, or 43,700yds (40,000m) at 38kt
   Warhead 1,080lbs (490kg)

HMS *Electra* was one of three British E-class destroyers attached to ABDA, after forming part of the ill-fated Force Z. *Electra* formed part of ABDA Striking Force at the Battle of the Java Sea, and fought a duel with Japanese destroyers, before being sunk, with the loss of 119 crewmen.

At the time, Doorman's cruisers were steaming in line ahead, with *De Ruyter* followed by *Exeter*, *Houston*, *Perth* and *Java*. The destroyers *Electra*, *Encounter* and *Jupiter* were ahead of them, in line abreast, while the Dutch destroyers *Kortenaer* and *Witte de With* were off the flagship's port quarter. The American destroyers *John D. Edwards*, *Alden*, *John D. Ford* and *Paul Jones* followed astern of the cruisers. Doorman was still steaming north-west, but when the firing began, he turned west, to allow his cruisers to fire.

By then, more enemy destroyers had been sighted to the north. *Nachi* and *Haguro* had also turned west on an almost parallel course to the Allies. In the gunnery duel that followed, Japanese gunnery proved effective, and *De Ruyter* was hit twice, although neither shell exploded. *Houston*'s rear turret was still out of commission, so each Allied heavy cruiser had only six 8in guns, to the ten on each of their Japanese counterparts.

Then from 1633hrs, for the next 19 minutes, the Japanese cruisers and seven destroyers launched a massed torpedo salvo at the Allied cruisers. The range was still about 15 miles – far too far away for a normal torpedo to have a chance of hitting the enemy. These though, were Type 93 Long Lance torpedoes, in use against the Allies for the first time. It came as a shock when these torpedoes arrived. At 1705hrs, *Exeter* was hit by one, but it didn't explode. Meanwhile, the range was closing and both sides were still firing. By 1708hrs, both *Exeter* and *Houston* had been hit, but only the British cruiser suffered a serious blow.

The Japanese 8in shell knocked out a boiler room, and the cruiser's speed dropped to 15kts. So, *Exeter* turned to port and pulled out of the Allied line. Unfortunately, the ships behind *Exeter* thought this was a planned manoeuvre and altered course too, so that apart from *De Ruyter*, all the Allied cruisers were heading towards the south-east, away from the enemy. Reluctantly, Doorman ordered *De Ruyter* to make the same turn, so that his cruiser force remained together. *Perth* also laid a smoke screen from the ship's funnels to hide *Exeter* from enemy fire. The sudden turn forced the accompanying Dutch destroyers to manoeuvre hard, to avoid colliding with the cruisers. That proved unfortunate for the rearmost destroyer *Kortenaer*, as at 1713hrs a torpedo from *Haguro* struck the ship amidships, ripping the hull apart. *Kortenaer* sank in less than two minutes.

After being damaged in the Flores Sea on 4 February, USS *Marblehead* limped into Tjilatjap on 6 February to land casualties and to patch the hole in the cruiser's bow, which would allow her flooded forward compartments to be pumped out. Here, casualties are stretchered ashore, for treatment in the port's hospital.

The initial Allied reaction was that these torpedoes had been launched by a submarine, as the Japanese surface ships were supposedly far beyond torpedo range. It slowly dawned that the Japanese torpedoes had a phenomenal range. Doorman decided to break off the action, to buy time for his cruisers to sort themselves out. So, he ordered the British destroyers to mount a counter-attack to cover the squadron's withdrawal. *Electra*, *Encounter* and *Jupiter* turned west and opened fire as soon as they emerged from the smoke screen. This was risky, as at that moment Japanese destroyers were racing in from the west, trying to outflank the Allied ships. Throughout all this, three floatplanes from Takagi's cruisers circled the area, correcting the fall of shot of the Japanese salvos.

By 1800hrs, the range had shortened markedly, and the British destroyers were coming under fire from Japanese destroyers of the 4th Flotilla, six miles to the south-west. Although the British destroyers scored hits, they were being badly pounded themselves, and *Electra* was soon crippled and left dead in the water. At that point Doorman recalled the British destroyers, and *Encounter* and *Jupiter* gratefully turned back to the east. *Electra* was finally finished off by the destroyer *Minegumo* at 1816hrs. Only 54 of *Electra*'s crew survived.

By 1800hrs, ABDA's cruisers had reformed their line and were steaming north-east, with *De Ruyter* in the lead. *Exeter* was four miles to the north, heading towards Sourabaya, while the American destroyers grouped off the cruisers' port beam laid smoke to cover the cruiser's withdrawal. Doorman hoped to break contact when night fell, but for the moment the Japanese were too close, with the heavy cruisers 12 miles to port, and the two destroyer flotillas 10 miles astern. At 1806hrs, to buy time, Doorman ordered the American destroyers to attack. He quickly cancelled this order, but the four old destroyers had already turned to face the enemy before they were recalled. They withdrew at 1817hrs, making smoke, after launching a 20-torpedo salvo.

Seeing this, *Nachi* and *Haguro* turned away, but the torpedoes lacked the range to reach them. This though, bought Doorman a little more time. However, Adm. Takagi then broke off the pursuit anyway, as his Japanese force was nearing the Java coast, and he didn't want to run into a Dutch minefield. For his part, despite losing two destroyers and almost a cruiser too, Doorman still hoped to intercept the Japanese transports. So, at 1831hrs, Doorman turned to the north-east, leaving *Exeter* to limp into Sourabaya.

Doorman's plan didn't consider the shadowing Japanese float planes. As darkness fell, both protagonists were heading north. Playing it safe, Takagi ordered the transports to withdraw north out of harm's way, while his Covering Force screened them from the Allies. At 2100hrs, Doorman turned west, as he continued his search for the Japanese transports. At that point the US destroyers broke off and returned to Sourabaya, as they were almost out of fuel. That left Doorman with just four cruisers (*De Ruyter*, *Houston*, *Java* and *Perth*) and the destroyer *Jupiter*. *Encounter* and *Witte de With* were far astern of Doorman's squadron. Doorman was still close to the Java coast though, and suddenly, at 2125hrs, *Jupiter* struck a stray Dutch mine, which wrecked the destroyer's engine room. The crippled vessel had to be left behind. *Jupiter* took four hours to sink, but the crew was able to abandon ship.

At 2150hrs, Doorman led his column of ships north again. At 2215hrs, they passed the survivors of *Kortenaer*, clinging to life rafts, near the scene of the afternoon's clash. *Encounter*, having recovered the 113 remaining survivors, while the rest of the Allied squadron steamed past, still searched for the enemy. Strangely, the Japanese were equally in the dark, as after their floatplanes landed to refuel, contact with the enemy was lost.

Then, at 2302hrs, lookouts aboard *Nachi* spotted the Allies' cruisers steering north, eight miles to the south-east. *Nachi* and *Haguro* were pointing south, so they turned onto a parallel course to the enemy. *Jintsu* and the destroyers of the 2nd Flotilla were four miles to the south-west of Takagi's flagship, and they too turned north. Eight minutes later, at 2310hrs, the Japanese cruisers were spotted by *De Ruyter*, and the Allies opened fire at a range of 4.5 miles. The Japanese returned fire with their 8in guns, but the two Japanese cruisers also launched a salvo of Type 93 torpedoes, eight from *Nachi* and four from *Haguro*. The range was seven miles. Meanwhile the gunnery duel continued.

Suddenly, at 2336hrs, an explosion rocked the stern of *Java*, on the port side. It was a torpedo hit, and the Dutch cruiser began to founder. The three remaining ABDA cruisers turned to starboard, to increase the range. Unfortunately for *De Ruyter*, this put Doorman's flagship directly into the path of one of *Haguro*'s torpedoes. Two minutes after *Java* had been torpedoed, an explosion erupted at the stern of *De Ruyter*. At first it seemed as if the detonation wasn't fatal. The cruiser was still level, but the blast had knocked out the ship's dynamos and started a fire, which rapidly engulfed the stern of the ship. Anti-aircraft ammunition began to 'cook off', adding to the conflagration.

When *De Ruyter* was hit, *Houston* and *Perth* were close by and had to turn sharply to avoid a collision. The crew of *Houston* saw torpedoes pass them on either beam, but both cruisers escaped being hit. Then they split up, heading to the south-east and north-east. A signal flashed from the flagship, an order for *Houston* and *Perth*: '*Do not stand by for survivors. Proceed to Batavia*.' So, the two remaining Allied cruisers broke off the action and withdrew to the south-east. The cruisers then came alongside each other, so that their captains could confer. They decided to make for Batavia at high speed. As a result, after the battle, ABDA still had something left with which to fight.

Back aboard *Java*, the tangled wreckage of the cruiser's stern was already underwater. Capt. van Straelen gave the order to abandon ship, but trouble finding stored lifejackets and launching the boats meant most of the crew had to jump overboard as they were. At 2352hrs, 15 minutes after being hit, *Java*'s bow rose up and the cruiser then slipped under the waves. In the end, only 19 of the cruiser's crew of 528 survived the sinking. On board *De Ruyter*, the loss of the dynamos meant that there was nothing to power the ship's fire hoses. So, the blaze spread. *De Ruyter* finally sank at 0230hrs on 28 February, with the loss of 344 of the cruiser's 435-man crew. R. Adm. Doorman went down with his ship.

Sunda Strait

At noon on Saturday 28 February *Houston* and *Perth* arrived in Tanjong Priok, the port serving Batavia, just over 300 miles from the scene of the disaster. Earlier that morning, the Eastern Striking Force had left port, bound for Ceylon by way of the Sunda Strait, the channel to the west of Java. Meanwhile, V. Adm. Takahashi's West Java Invasion Force was heading towards Bantam Bay, 40 miles to the west of Batavia. It was escorted by two destroyer flotillas, and screened by R. Adm. Kurita's Covering Force of four heavy cruisers, the light carrier *Ryujo* and seven more destroyers. So, if they stayed, *Perth*, *Houston* and

THE BATTLE OF THE JAVA SEA, FRIDAY 27 FEBRUARY 1942

On 26 February, as the Japanese launched their invasion of Java, R. Adm. Doorman put to sea from Sourabaya in an attempt to intercept the Japanese transport fleet in the Java Sea, before it could reach the Dutch-owned island. Instead, they were detected by the Japanese, and late the next afternoon, at 1548hrs, rather than a transport fleet they encountered a powerful Japanese surface group. During the opening clashes of the battle the Japanese made liberal use of their Type 93 Long Lance torpedoes, and although only one hit a target, the Allies were aghast that these torpedoes had such an extensive range – double that of their own.

Doorman did what he could to hold off the Japanese until sunset, when he might have a chance to disengage. By 1735hrs, when this view is set, the Allied cruisers HNLMS *De Ruyter*, USS *Houston* and HMS *Exeter* had all been damaged, and the destroyer HNLMS *Kortenaer* had been sunk. It was the damage to *Exeter* though, greatly reducing the cruiser's speed, that forced Doorman to take drastic action. He ordered his American and Dutch destroyers to lay smoke, to cover the withdrawal of his cruisers, while the British destroyers HMS *Electra*, HMS *Encounter* and HMS *Jupiter* made a feint towards the enemy, to delay pursuit. Leading the line of cruisers here is HMAS *Perth*. The line of smoke-laying destroyers is off their port beam, and the Japanese are approaching from their starboard quarter.

In the end Doorman's attempt proved unsuccessful, and his fleet paid the price. During the battle, both *Electra* and *Jupiter* were lost, together with two Allied cruisers.

the Dutch destroyer *Evertsen* would be trapped. Some 350 miles to the east, in Sourabaya, the destroyers *Encounter* and *Witte de With* were still there, as were the US destroyers *Alden, John D. Edwards, John D. Ford, Paul Jones* and *Pope* of US Destroyer Division 59.

It was now clear that Adm. Helfrich's attempt to defend Java had failed. It was time to save whatever warships could escape through waters which were now controlled by the Japanese. At 1900hrs on Saturday evening, *Houston* and *Perth* left port and headed west towards the Sunda Strait. Almost two hours later, *Evertsen* followed them to sea. The Japanese landings began at 0200hrs on Sunday 1 March, but with unusual laxity, as the Japanese hadn't expected an Allied force to appear from the east. Meanwhile, at 2230hrs on Saturday evening, *Perth* and *Houston* approached the seaward side of Bantam Bay, making 28kts.

Only one destroyer, *Fubuki*, was stationed to the east of the landing zone, off Babi Island. The transports lying in the bay were protected by two more destroyers, while the bulk of the Japanese force lay to the west, covering the entrance to the Sunda Strait. The Japanese deployment that evening was poorly managed, but then again, the chances of the invading force encountering any serious naval opposition were slim. However, *Fubuki* at least was in the right place, and the destroyer's crew sighted the two approaching cruisers at 2239hrs and duly raised the alarm.

Capt. Waller of *Perth*, who commanded the two Allied ships, ordered his yeoman to signal the dark shape ahead, as he'd been told Dutch patrol boats were there, guarding the entrance to the Strait. The response signal flashed back by *Fubuki* was incorrect, revealing the vessel was an enemy one. *Fubuki* then turned away, making smoke, while to the south, another destroyer (*Harukaze*) appeared, heading west, also making smoke. Moments later, Waller saw what

A depiction of the sinking of the cruiser USS *Houston* at some point between 0030 hrs and 0035hrs on 1 March 1942, during the Battle of Sunda Strait. By then the cruiser had taken four torpedo hits and numerous shell hits from encircling Japanese destroyers. (Copy of original artwork by Joe Fleischmann, in the US Navy Art Collection)

the destroyer was trying to hide. *Houston* fired a starshell, which revealed a fleet of transport ships at anchor 12 miles away, off the western entrance to the bay. In all there were 27 transports there, lying off the coast. Unknown to the Allies, over to the west various groups of Japanese warships turned and headed towards this unexpected threat. Most were destroyers, but among them were the heavy cruisers *Mikuma* and *Mogami*.

Adm. Doorman knew not to surprise a Japanese transport fleet before it had a chance to land its troops. The two cruisers though, had little chance of inflicting damage to the transports, as by then small groups of Japanese destroyers were beginning to appear out of the darkness ahead of them. On the bridge of *Perth*, Waller was heard to say: '*It looks like a bit of a trap*.' It wasn't, as the Japanese had been taken unawares. However, given the odds facing the two Allied ships, it would soon become one. At 2314hrs *Fubuki*, shadowing the enemy cruisers, turned and launched a salvo of nine torpedoes. There was little chance of a hit, and sure enough *Houston* and *Perth* were spared. However, what followed was a somewhat haphazard response by the Japanese. *Fubuki* fired nine torpedoes at the Allied cruisers, all of them missed, due mainly to the poor angle between the firer and its two targets. Meanwhile, almost all of the Japanese cruisers and destroyers cruising to the west of Bantam Bay then headed towards the Allied cruisers, in response to *Fubuki*'s alert. Two more destroyers steamed north out of the bay itself, while the two Japanese heavy cruisers headed south-east at full speed to intercept the enemy. Meanwhile, moments after circling to port to avoid *Fubuki*'s torpedoes, Waller decided to close the range with the transports. *Perth* and *Houston* then headed towards the south-west, towards Panjang Island, at the mouth of the bay. *Harukaze*, one of the two destroyers in Bantam Bay, had

THE BATTLE OF THE SUNDA STRAIT, SUNDAY 1 MARCH 1942

Late on 28 February, the heavy cruiser USS *Houston* and light cruiser HMAS *Perth* were ordered to leave Batavia and transit the Sunda Strait to reach a safer port. Intelligence reports suggested that there were no Japanese warships in the area. However, unbeknown to the Allies, a Japanese invasion fleet had reached Bantam Bay, near the north-west tip of Java. So just after 2300hrs the following evening, as the two Allied cruisers were passing to the north of the bay, a ship was sighted. It was the Japanese destroyer *Harukaze*. It wasn't alone.

On spotting the Japanese transports, Capt. Waller of *Perth* requested *Houston* join him in an attack. However, Japanese destroyers soon appeared, singly or in small groups, and the Allied cruisers were encircled. When the destroyers fired at them, the Allies replied. The destroyers also launched multiple torpedo salvos, which somehow *Houston* and *Perth* avoided – for now. This shows the situation at 2345hrs, when the two cruisers had turned west to fight their way through to the Sunda Strait. To port is the destroyer *Hatakaze*, while to starboard are *Hatsuyuki*, *Shirayuki* and *Fubuki*. Ahead, *Harukaze* is laying smoke to screen the transports, while the destroyers *Asakaze* and *Shiratsuyu* are also engaging the Allies. Further off are two more destroyers, *Murakumo* and *Shirakumo*. Minutes later, the Japanese heavy cruisers *Mikuma* and *Mogami* appeared, and any hope the Allies had would be snatched away. The battle ended with the loss of both Allied cruisers.

A depiction of the crew of a Japanese 21in torpedo mount, launching a salvo of Type 93 torpedoes at USS *Houston* during the Sunda Strait battle. The firer is one of the four Kamikaze-class destroyers present that night, all of which mounted three power-operated mountings, each of two torpedo tubes.

turned to the north-west, laying smoke to screen its valuable charges.

Afterwards, to cover up some of the chaos of the night-time encounter, the Japanese claimed they had intended to lure the two Allied cruisers into their midst, but in reality, this whole engagement was an impromptu one with no real plan on either side. At around 2325hrs, after the torpedo salvo from *Fubuki* had been sidestepped, Waller spotted a flotilla of Japanese destroyers to the north-east, astride their direct route to the Sunda Strait and safety. *Perth* was already engaging *Harukaze* to the south-west, but this posed a much more serious threat. Waller turned his cruisers a little to port, and headed west, while both cruisers brought their guns to bear. Meanwhile, the Japanese destroyers *Hatsuyuki* and *Shirayuki* closed in for a torpedo attack. A 6in shell from *Perth* struck the bridge of *Shirayuki*, but the Japanese destroyers kept on course, watched by the light cruiser *Natori*, the flagship of V. Adm. Hara's 5th Destroyer Division.

The two destroyers launched a nine-torpedo salvo at a range of just two miles, then turned away. *Perth* and *Houston* dodged these, but by then the rest of Hara's destroyers had appeared and began their own torpedo runs. *Hatsukaze*, *Asakaze* and *Harukaze* all opened fire first and a gunnery duel developed, as searchlights from both sides swept over the water. *Harukaze* was hit several times, and veered off, but *Asakaze* launched six torpedoes at the enemy cruisers, from a range of three miles. *Natori* fired four more, even though the light cruiser was heading away from the enemy cruisers. The time was now 2343hrs. Waller ordered his two cruisers to turn away to port, then settled on a reciprocal easterly course. So far though, *Perth* and *Houston* had avoided any serious damage. Their luck though, couldn't last, as yet more Japanese destroyers were sighted to the north and the north-west.

It was a chaotic sight, with gunfire, torpedo tracks and searchlight beams all seemingly following the two cruisers and the clusters of destroyers. Starshells also pierced the darkness, lighting up *Houston* and *Perth* for all to see. At that point at 2346hrs, R. Adm. Kurita had caught sight of the enemy cruisers five miles to the south. He ordered the destroyers to clear the area, and steered east, to allow the full 8in batteries of his heavy cruisers *Mikuma* and *Mogami* to bear. He also launched a spread of six torpedoes from each cruiser, but these went wide of their targets. At 2352hrs, the two Japanese cruisers switched on their searchlights and opened fire. *Houston* and *Perth* returned fire, aiming at the searchlights, and at 2355hrs *Mikuma* was hit.

The two Allied cruisers were doing well, but they were now down to their last few shells – *Perth* was even reduced to using starshells and practice rounds. For their part, the crew of *Houston* formed a human chain to manhandle 8in shells forward from her disabled after turret. It was all very courageous, but it couldn't last. On V. Adm. Hara's orders the Japanese destroyers closed in again. While the inner group of *Hatsuyuki*, *Shirayuki*, *Hatakaze*, *Asakaze* and *Harukaze* closed in from the north and north-west, around two miles from the Allied ships, other destroyers – *Shirakumo*, *Murakumo* and *Shiratsuyu* – a little further off approached from the west. Even *Fubuki* a little to the north was eager to attack again.

After encountering the escorts of a Japanese invasion fleet near the Sunda Strait, HMAS *Perth* and USS *Houston* were attacked and sunk by the Japanese escort force. Here, the crippled *Houston* is shown just before midnight on 28 February, pinned by searchlights and encircled by destroyers. (Copy of original painting by John Hamilton)

At 2356hrs *Harukaze* and *Hatakaze* fired 11 torpedoes between them, and a minute later the cruiser *Mogami*, five miles to the north launched five more. Two and a half miles to the west, *Shirakumo* and *Murakumo* launched nine torpedoes between them, and even Hara's flagship, the light cruiser *Natori*, joined in by launching another five torpedoes from a range of over four miles. With 30 torpedoes heading towards *Houston* and *Perth* from multiple directions, avoiding them seemed impossible. Amazingly though, despite several very near misses, the two Allied cruisers evaded most of the onslaught. The transport fleet though, was less fortunate. From 0005hrs, on what was Sunday 1 March, four torpedoes hit transport ships in Bantam Bay, and all the crippled ships sank. So too did the minesweeper *W2*, which took a direct hit. However, at the same moment that a torpedo struck the first transport *Ryujo Maru*, another torpedo finally dealt *Perth* a mortal blow.

It struck the cruiser's starboard side, between the boiler room and forward engine room. *Perth* took on water, exacerbating the effect of an earlier waterline hit, and the helm began to stop responding correctly. Capt. Waller ordered his crew to prepare to abandon ship, while damage-control parties tried to stem the flood. Then, two minutes later, *Perth* was struck by two more torpedoes, beneath 'A' turret forward, and 'X' turret aft. As the cruiser began to settle, Waller ordered his crew to abandon ship, then remained on the bridge as his ship sank beneath him. As *Perth* was sinking, destroyers closed in and poured in more shells from their guns, and at least one more torpedo. At 0025hrs, *Perth* finally sank, together with 351 of the ship's crew.

Meanwhile *Houston*, 'Galloping Ghost of the Java Coast', was fighting on. It was clear now that escape was impossible, and the cruiser was pinned in the glare of half a dozen searchlights. *Mikuma* and *Mogami* had closed the range and were pounding *Houston*, while the Americans' fire slackened as the last rounds were used up. At about 0010hrs, *Houston* took a serious hit on the starboard side, wrecking the after engine room, and the cruiser's speed dropped. Then, a hit on 'No 2' ('B') turret started a major fire, which forced Capt. Rooks to order the forward magazines to be flooded. *Houston* was now virtually defenceless. The cruiser's secondary 5in guns were reduced to firing starshells. The end came suddenly, at around 0020hrs. The cruiser was struck almost simultaneously by three or four torpedoes, the first on the starboard side beneath the bridge, then others further aft on the same side.

Houston began listing to starboard, so Rooks ordered a marine bugler to sound the call to abandon ship. The Japanese were still firing as the crew jumped into the sea. Capt. Rooks was hit by shrapnel as he waited his turn, and died on the deck of his cruiser. The final moments of *Houston* were illuminated by the Japanese searchlights, as the burning, battered hull rolled over to starboard, helped along at 0029hrs by a final torpedo hit on the port beam as the ship sunk. Although sources disagree, official US Navy records put the time of sinking at approximately 0043hrs. Of *Houston*'s crew of 1,061, a total of 693 died that evening. Later, at least another 100 American and as many Australian sailors died in Japanese prison camps. It was a bloody end to the last remaining fully operational cruisers in ABDA's Striking Force.

Second Java Sea

Even with the loss of *Houston* and *Perth*, there were still several ABDA warships trapped in Java with no clear way out. In Sourabaya, Cdr Binford still had the four old destroyers of the US Navy's Destroyer Division 58, his own *John. D. Edwards*, as well as *Alden*, *John D. Ford* and *Paul Jones*. He decided to escape by way of the Bali Strait, around the east of Java. So, at 1700hrs on 28 February, the four destroyers slipped out of Sourabaya and steamed east. Nine hours later at 0200hrs they entered the Bali Strait, which was patrolled by four Japanese, destroyers. Binford though, hugged the Java coast, trying to slip past them in the dark. However, they were spotted and the enemy destroyers gave chase and opened fire. The American destroyers returned fire, but for some reason the Japanese didn't pursue them for long and turned back to their original patrol line. Perhaps they felt the obsolete destroyers weren't worth it and were waiting for a more prestigious opponent. Binford's destroyers eventually reached Freemantle in Western Australia on 4 March.

This view, taken from a Japanese floatplane, shows the final moments of the British heavy cruiser HMS *Exeter* on 1 March, during the Second Battle of the Java Sea. Capt. Gordon ordered his crew to abandon ship when the cruiser lost all power and was unable to fight.

That still left the damaged British cruiser *Exeter* in Sourabaya, together with the destroyers *Encounter* and *Pope*. Owing to the cruiser's draft, it was felt that only the Sunda Strait was navigable, even though the chances of making it safely around Java by the westward route were slim. *Exeter* and the two destroyers left port at 1900hrs on 28 February – two hours after Binford – and steamed west up Java's north coast. Their departure though, was spotted by Japanese aircraft, depriving Capt. Gordon of *Exeter* of any element of surprise. At 2330hrs, word reached *Exeter* that *Houston* and *Perth* were in action off the entrance to the Sunda Strait. At that point Gordon should have reversed course and tried to make it out by another route, such as the Bali or Lombok Strait. At that point Gordon's force was in the Java Sea, east of Bawean Island, and heading north, to avoid Japanese patrols, before heading through the Sunda Strait.

When dawn came, on Sunday 1 March they were 60 miles off the southern coast of Borneo, steaming west through calm seas and under a clear, cloudless sky. At 0750hrs, ships were sighted. They were part of Adm. Takahashi's Covering Force, the heavy cruisers *Ashigara* and *Myoko*, and the destroyers *Akebono* and *Ikazuchi*. Gordon turned east, but his force was gradually overhauled, and, at 1020hrs, his three ships came under fire from the Japanese cruisers at a range of 12 miles. Accuracy was aided by a Japanese float plane, which directed the cruisers' fall of shot. *Exeter*, short of ammunition, fought back, and even launched torpedoes, but it wasn't enough. By 1115hrs, the heavy cruisers *Nachi* and *Haguro* had joined the fight, together with two more destroyers, *Kamakaze* and *Yamakaze*. *Exeter* was hit repeatedly, and at 1120hrs an 8in shell struck the boiler room and the cruiser lost power. The pounding continued though, until 1145hrs, when the cruiser was struck by two torpedoes. Gordon ordered his crew to abandon ship, and *Exeter* capsized and sank five minutes later.

Another view of the damaged British heavy cruiser HMS *Exeter* sinking in the Java Sea a little after noon on 1 March, after being ambushed and beaten by a powerful Japanese surface force. In all, 652 of *Exeter*'s crew including Capt. Gordon were rescued by the Japanese destroyer IJNS *Inadzuma*, and so became prisoners of war.

As for the destroyers, at 1135hrs, *Encounter* was damaged by an 8in shell, and the destroyer lost all power. Lt Cdr Morgan gave the order to abandon ship, and the destroyer was then scuttled. Most of the crew of the two British warships were rescued and taken prisoner. As for *Pope*, the American destroyer managed to escape under cover of a rain squall, but at 1300hrs the fleeing destroyer was sighted by Japanese aircraft. Lt Cdr Blinn avoided several bombing attacks, but near misses damaged the propeller shaft and flooding took hold. The crew had abandoned *Pope*, and the ship was being scuttled when *Myoko* and *Ashigara* appeared. The destroyer sank at 1420hrs, and again the survivors were duly rescued. Apart from Gordon's three-ship force, there were other ABDA warships trapped in Java. The destroyers *Edsall* and *Pillsbury* left Tjilatjap on 28 February, but they were sunk in the Indian Ocean to the south-east of Java by battleships and cruisers 200 miles east of Christmas Island on 1 March and 2 March respectively. There were no survivors, save for 34 from *Edsall*, who were executed by the Japanese. Only the American destroyers *Parrott* and *Whipple* successfully escaped from Java, and reached Australia.

ANALYSIS

ABDA Striking Force was created five weeks after the Japanese launched their offensive in South-East Asia. By then, the Philippines had fallen as had Hong Kong, British Borneo and much of Malaya. A few days before, Tarakan off Dutch Borneo and Menado in the Celebes had also fallen. Britain's Force Z had been sunk and the US Asiatic Fleet had been driven out of the Philippines. Everywhere the Japanese enjoyed numerical superiority at sea and in the air. It is hard to think of worse conditions for the forging of a new military and naval alliance.

The ad-hoc naval command, formed from whatever was to hand from four navies was ill-prepared. While the Americans, British, Dutch and Australians had some modern warships in their contingents, other warships were little short of liabilities in a modern naval war. Most ships were poorly armed in comparison with the Japanese warships facing them.

Supply and maintenance problems dogged ABDA as all but the Dutch were operating without naval bases of their own. This meant they were often short of fuel and ordnance. Near the end, in the Battle of the Sunda Strait, USS *Houston* and HMAS *Perth* were reduced to firing practice or illumination rounds at the enemy. Even the Dutch were suffering as since the fall of the Netherlands, no supplies of any kind had reached the East Indies. They had begun manufacturing their own shells and stockpiling fuel produced in Dutch East Indies refineries. However, this wasn't enough.

Another problem was the naval command structure. Each of the constituent navies had its own system of command, so R. Adm. Doorman answered to his Dutch superior, V. Adm. Helfrich, as well as his operational superior, Adm. Hart. Both commanders gave him operational orders or advice, which were sometimes at odds. None of these three naval commanders had a full understanding of the Japanese threat. Throughout the campaign ABDA was also poorly served by its intelligence gathering.

Of the seven major engagements ABDA Striking Force took part in, only one, Balikpapan, could be considered a victory. Of the others, two were air attacks which betrayed their limited anti-aircraft capability. The other engagements ended in the loss of or damage to ships, without gaining any advantage. The last two engagements were little more than slaughters. Both Doorman and his superiors made errors of judgement, but ultimately their decisions made little difference. Even if more air support had been available, it is unlikely Doorman could have stemmed the Japanese tide. The disparity was simply too great; the Japanese were able to carry out amphibious landings before the Allies

The sinking of the seaplane carrier USS *Langley* (CV-1) in the Indian Ocean, 70 miles south of the Javanese port of Tjilatjap. At 1140hrs, *Langley* was attacked by 16 Japanese Betty bombers and took five hits, leaving the ship dead in the water. At 1429hrs, *Langley* was scuttled by escorting destroyers. In this view taken from the USS *Whipple*, the USS *Edsall* can be seen off the carrier's port side after taking off survivors.

truly realized what was afoot. By late February, once all of Java was within range of Japanese aircraft, it was simply a matter of time before ABDA was defeated.

In the end, all ABDA Striking Force achieved was to delay the Japanese invasion of Java. Without recognizing the dangers of Japanese militarism, the fate of ABDA was sealed before the war began.

This Japanese photograph taken from the cruiser IJMS *Tone* in the Indian Ocean south-west of Java shows the Clemson-class destroyer USS *Edsall* under fire from a Japanese surface force. This included two battleships, which fired almost 300 14in shells at the destroyer. This salvo actually lifted *Edsall*'s bows out of the water. After a later air attack, *Edsall* finally sank at 1731hrs on 1 March. The eight survivors were subsequently beheaded by their captors.

If there was one bright note to take away from the story, it was the ability of the Allies to forge an ad-hoc military alliance in the face of a major external threat. On 4 April 1949, just over eight years after the collapse of ABDA, another similar multi-national alliance was formed. The North Atlantic Treaty Organization (NATO) relied on the idea of the collective security of its members, much as ABDA did. It has been one of the great success stories of the post-war world. With ABDA, four navies fought against a common foe. NATO though, has been in existence for almost eight decades, and so has had time to work out any teething problems. ABDA didn't have that luxury. If anything, the fate of ABDA serves as a demonstration of the importance of international cooperation, and a united military resolve.

FURTHER READING

Bioer, P.C., *The Loss of Java*, University of Singapore Press, Singapore, 2011

Cain, T.J. & A.L. Selwood, *HMS Electra*, Frederick Muller, London, 1959

Chesneau, Roger (ed.), *Conway's All the World's Fighting Ships, 1922–1946*, Conway Maritime Press, London, 1980

Cox, Jeffrey R., *Rising Sun, Falling Skies: The Disastrous Java Sea Campaign of World War II*, Osprey Publishing, Oxford, 2014

Gordon, Oliver, *Fight it Out*, William Kimber, London, 1957

McKie, Ronald, *Proud Echo*, Robert Hale, London, 1954

Morison, Samuel Eliot, *History of the United States Naval Operations in World War II, Vol. III: the Rising Sun in the Pacific, 1931–April 1942*, Little, Brown & Co., Boston MA, 1988

Osten, F.C. van, *The Battle of the Java Sea* (Sea Battles in Close-Up Series), Ian Allan Ltd, London, 1976

Roskill, S.W., *The War at Sea, Vol. II. The Period of Balance* (History of the Second World War Series), HMSO, London, 1952

Thomas, David A., *Battle of the Java Sea*, André Deutsch, London, 1968

Winslow, Walter G., *The Fleet the Gods Forgot*, Naval Institute Press, Annapolis, 1984

INDEX

Figures in **bold** refer to photos and illustrations.